# Vision, Valleys
# & Victories:

## Growing Liberia International

## Christian College

# Vision, Valleys & Victories:

## Growing Liberia International Christian College

**Dr. Sei Buor**

WITH MARK OEHLER

# Dedication

This book is dedicated to our friend and pastor,

**Rev. Paul Thompson**

The Senior Pastor of
Northwest Covenant Church in Mount Prospect, Illinois.

He and his church have been great supporters of my family
and of Liberia International Christian College.
He has visited the campus and been a great encouragement.

In December 2014 Paul was diagnosed with lung cancer,
and I was with him and his family recently
for his last chemotherapy.

The purpose of dedicating the book to Pastor Paul is
so all our friends who read this book will remember
to pray for our dear friend to be cancer-free.

Rev. Paul Thompson and his wife, Mary, with Sei

# Table of Contents

# Preface

Many of you know my history and that of ULICAF and LICC because you know me personally, or have heard me speak, or you are familiar with my first book, *NO MORE WAR*. Other readers may be less familiar with this history. To both sets of readers, I would like to give a brief background to provide a common understanding of where I came from and why I have been so motivated to see LICC come to fruition.

The pursuit of education has defined my life. Education was a passion for me from a very early age. I was born and grew up in the small village of Yarsonnoh (Riverview), Nimba County, Liberia. My first education was tribal as was that of my contemporaries. We learned how to survive in the jungle in the Poro School. We learned how to make clothing; how to build a shelter from branches and tree leaves; how to find, gather, and cook food; how to dig a well, and many other things that were necessary for survival without modern conveniences in the jungle. We also learned subsistence farming from our families.

I wanted more education than that. I desperately wanted to go to elementary school. With my father's help, I was fortunate to attend Karnwee Elementary school. This was the beginning of my western-style education. My "commute" to this school was walking 5 miles each way on dirt roads.

Through a series of circumstances, at age 10, I was able to attend the Cocopa Plantation School to complete my grade school. This private school was a vast improvement in opportunity for me. After grade school, I desired to go to high school. There were no local high school, so I ended up attending St. Samuels High School outside of my region. Eventually, I was able to attend Sanniquellie Central High School, the best public high school available in Nimba County.

It was shortly after my time there that I came to know the saving power of Jesus Christ. I am eternally thankful to Dr. Amos Miamen and his wife

Mary who shared this knowledge with me and mentored me as I grew in faith.

In 1981 I started teaching at United Liberia Inland Church Academy (a high school). I learned to share the gospel under the tutelage of Rev. "Pop" Carson and served as a translator for visiting evangelists.

In 1982, I started my college education by attending African Bible College (ABC), now ABC University. Upon graduation, I returned to teaching and pastoring a local church. Yah and I started our family, and Yah continued her small business to help support our family.

Sei and Yah's Young Family

My next educational pursuit was at an East African college with an international reputation: Nairobi Evangelical Graduate School of Theology (NEGST) in Nairobi, Kenya. The institution is now called Africa International University (AIU). Getting there was difficult financially, but we eventually did get there, and I earned a Master of Divinity. During this time, both Yah and I worked small businesses to help support our family.

When I graduated, civil war had broken out in Liberia. I was unable to safely return my family to Liberia and so I ended up taking a position as a pastor in Gambia with the help of World Evangelization for Christ International (WEC Int'l). While in Gambia, I began to pursue further education in the United States. I was accepted to Western Theological Seminary in Holland, Michigan. Before I left for America, I wanted to return to Liberia to visit my family and to observe conditions there. Many counseled against this, but I did manage to visit, and I did return safely after seeing the devastation and bidding farewell to my mother.

In 1994, I flew to the United States to commence my education at Western Theological Seminary. Eventually, with the help of a local church, Christ Memorial Church, I was able to bring my family to Holland, Michigan, to live with me as I continued my education in 1995. Both Yah and I worked several jobs, including working on a blueberry farm, to support our family during our time in Holland.

When I graduated from Western Theological Seminary, the civil war was still raging, and it was considered unsafe to return. I did not know what to do and was tired of education. However, God had a plan for me and I was accepted to Loyola University in Chicago.

Ultimately, my Doctorate from Loyola is the pinnacle of my educational career. I am very proud, yet humbled, that they accepted me as a student. Loyola is a prestigious school with an international reputation beyond religious education; they also have educated many evangelical leaders. I am even happier to have done the work necessary to earn my Doctorate in Educational Leadership and Policy Studies.

Sei's Graduation from Loyola

Both Yah and I worked as we waited for a time when it would be safe to return to Liberia. For a while, I was a teaching assistant in the Indianapolis school district where I worked with disadvantaged children with learning disabilities.

I co-founded of the United Liberia Inland Church and Friends (ULICAF) in 1996. This group of mostly displaced Liberians worked hard to help fellow Liberians establish themselves and learn the culture of the United States. Most are Christians and feel that an education is very important.

In 2005, I accepted a full-time ministry position with ULICAF as Executive Director. Members of ULICAF felt that Liberia needs more educated people to establish itself as a self-governing country and to meet the many needs of the people. As a result, in 2008 I became co-founder and President of Liberia International Christian College (LICC) in Ganta, Liberia. My studies at Loyola strengthened me and gave me the background I needed as I helped design the plan to develop Liberia International Christian College. LICC is considered by many to be the first indigenous Christian college in West Africa. In this role, I am uniquely able to speak about the long and often faith-testing path God led the friends and associates of ULICAF on as they built LICC from the bare ground up.

If a leader is married, and if his commitment to his organization is to be strong, he or she needs the strong support of the spouse. I am grateful that my wife has been supportive of me throughout our long, sometimes arduous, journey. Without her active support, this journey of leading an organization to build a college in Liberia would have been very difficult and maybe impossible. There are people I know who do not have their spouses' support. It is difficult for them to accomplish even a part of their dream. Thankfully, Yah has stood with me through it all.

Again, if you would like to know more of my history, I would encourage you to read my first book, *NO MORE WAR: Rebuilding Liberia through Faith, Determination & Education.*

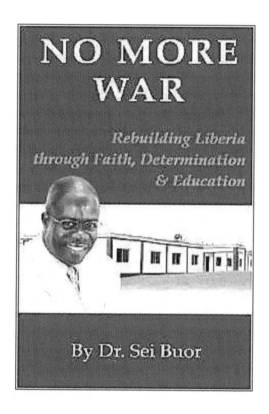

# Introduction

## *From a Dream to a Reality*

A passion for education has been a defining feature of my life. Given that, it should not be too much of a surprise that one of the most rewarding days of my life was a college graduation day. What may be somewhat surprising is that I am not talking about one of my own graduations or the graduation of any of my children,

No, the graduation day that meant the most to me was the day the first students graduated from Liberian International Christian College (LICC)! We at ULICAF (United Liberia Inland Church & Friends) had finally accomplished our goal in founding and establishing an institution of higher learning in Liberia.

It had been a long journey, together with many other people who sacrificed financially and gave of their time and prayers to a cause they felt worthy of sacrifice. For me that journey started in Liberia where I walked those five long miles each day to my first school. Since then, I completed high school, Bible College, seminary, and then two advanced degrees in America. I have taught school; I have pastored churches; I have evangelized my village. I met and married my wife and raised a family. I wrote one book and you hold in your hands the second book I have written.

As I pursued my passion for education, I found myself transitioning from pursuing education for myself to an intense desire to see others have opportunities for education. To that end, I have dedicated decades of my life and professional career to advancing the educational opportunities available to students in Liberia. My experiences have shown me over and over again the importance and impact of a Christ-centered education.

My wife and I were amongst the visionary leaders of ULICAF who began their ministry in America to help fellow refugees. We started by helping them to settle in their new culture and community in America. From that humble beginning developed the seed of an idea that would be Liberian International Christian College. Our goal with LICC was daunting and inspiring at the same time: we wanted to train transformative Christian leaders. Liberia International Christian College was to be a *higher education learning community committed to helping students develop in mind, spirit and body for a life of service to Christ in the Church and the World.*

LICC was started with the intention to graduate Christian leaders with a global perspective who are competent, caring, creative, generous individuals of character and potential. We are striving to build programs that will enable each member of the college to become stronger in body, mind, and spirit and to experience what it means to love God and your neighbor.

God has blessed our efforts. Since the launching of LICC in 2009, we have experienced a miracle which has resulted in extraordinary growth and change. We have built new buildings, created new academic programs, seen enrollment grow, and even added 4.5 acres to our campus for a total of 24.5 acres. In January 2016 we plan to begin work on our community health center.

Yes, without doubt, we have witnessed miraculous changes, but we shouldn't be too surprised, as we are building on a solid faith foundation. The values of the leaders of ULICAF in America and the leaders of the United Liberian Inland Church (ULIC) in Liberia have guided our actions from the beginning, and they continue to shape our academic and co-curriculum programs, our buildings and most importantly, our faculty, staff, donors, and students.

One of our recent achievements was dedicating a state-of-the-art modern Community Research Center (Library and Technology Center). In 2010,

Her Excellency, President Ellen Johnson-Sirleaf, led us in the groundbreaking ceremony for the CRC. It took four focused, hardworking years, to complete the project, but, with God's help, we did. The CRC was dedicated, **Sunday, July 6, 2014**! However, that was not the greatest happening at LICC that day. That day we also graduated 35 more candidates. It was our third graduation!

Every day belongs to God. What we do personally and collectively today will determine largely the tomorrow of all who share in it. Today, we are together on a journey that will place Liberia International Christian College among the great Christian colleges in Liberia and beyond. Our impact will multiply as students from LICC bring to the people of Liberia their Christian dedication and skills.

I look forward to seeing the impact of those trained at LICC in Liberia and in the world. I hope one day to write a book about their impact on the world. I long to see how they will share what they have learned with the next generation, and we will know that what we sacrificed for LICC was not in vain.

Although our race is not over, we have come a long way. Please join me as I share the vision and the many valleys and victories of this journey so far.

# Chapter 1: The Civil War

## A Brief History

Almost all current adult Liberians were affected by the civil war. Although my mother, my wife, our children, and I survived, my father and several of my brothers were killed as were many, many more people that I personally knew.

The war raged, with only a few interspersed months of relative peace, for 14 years. The population of Liberia was about three million before the war. Almost 250,000 Liberians were killed during the civil war, which is about 1 out of 12 Liberians. An estimated one million Liberians were displaced into neighboring countries for at least some part of the civil war.

Many Liberians, if they are willing to talk about the civil war at length, share their stories of "surviving" it. They do this for a reason. Even those who survived the war suffered emotional scars and tremendous losses—the loss of home, the loss of livelihood, the loss of family members, and the loss of great lifelong friends. Some continue to experience overwhelming guilt because they directly caused great suffering for others. Whether they were a victim or a perpetrator, they may have come out alive, but they did not come through unscathed.

In my first book, *NO MORE WAR: Rebuilding Liberia through Faith, Determination & Education* (available on Amazon), I recounted the story of my visit to Liberia to see friends and family before starting my studies at Western Theological Seminary in Holland, Michigan in the United States. This was during the civil war. I had surreptitiously entered the country. I went to the village where I grew up and found it demolished, abandoned, and literally retaken by the jungle foliage. I was unable to learn where my father was buried or if he had had the dignity of a burial. I shared about my visit with my mom in the bush where the survivors of my village hid to escape further attack. I did not delve into this deeply. Even to think back on it now is painful.

In this book, I am going to share a little more about the civil war to help you better understand the atmosphere we were working in when we started Liberia International Christian College (LICC) and initiated our ministry of helping our native country rebuild. I realize that some of this will be painful to my Liberian readers. Nonetheless, I think you will find in the end, as I have, hope rising from the ashes of that destruction. God will work good out of even the worst of evils and suffering—if we let Him.

First, I will provide a little history for those who are unfamiliar with Liberia. Liberia was founded by the United States as a place for freed slaves to live when they returned to Africa. The first freed Africans returned in 1820 to lands purchased with the help of the American Colonization Society (ACS). Indeed, the capital city Monrovia is named after James Monroe, the United States President who actively helped the ACS.

Liberia was granted its independence from the United States on July 26, 1847. At that time, its citizens were a combination of returned slaves and people indigenous to the region. As an independent country, the Liberian government was based on the United States model. Because of this, Liberia is generally considered Africa's first independent republic.

For the first century or more, the Liberian economy and politics were dominated by the returned slaves, referred to as the "Congo" people, or Americo-Liberians. In 1971, President Tolbert, an Americo-Liberian, worked to improve relations between the Americo-Liberians and the "Country people" who were the indigenous ethnic groups. Many in his party, the True Whig Party (TWP) felt he moved too fast; many activists felt he was moving too slowly.

President William R. Tolbert, Jr. (from Wikipedia)

An increase in the price of rice (rice is the staple Liberian food) then led to riots. Many of the indigenous people felt left out or pushed aside. They looked for a "savior." Unfortunately, a human savior was found.

On April 3, 1980, Tolbert was assassinated. Samuel Doe, an indigenous Liberian, and the People's Redemption Council (PRC) took control of the country. They promised to make things better for the indigenous peoples, but those promises were not fulfilled.

Samuel Kanyon Doe

Instead, Liberia turned into a dictatorship run by Doe. In 1985, Doe won re-election, but conditions worsened. Tension among the 16 Liberian tribes was exacerbated. Many believe that the PRC used the tension throughout the country to keep Liberians from uniting against the administration.

Charles M. Taylor

Among those who fled the country during Doe's presidency was the Americo-Liberian Charles Taylor. Accused of embezzling money from the Liberian government, he initially fled to the United States and then proceeded to Libya. On December 24, 1989, Charles Taylor returned to Liberia as the head of an army which contained many ex-members of the Armed Forces of Liberia (AFL). Thus began 14 years of brutal civil war among a number of warlords and the government. The war was marked with ethnic cleansing and brutality toward civilians. The first civil war (1989–1996) was started by Charles Taylor and other warlords who fought against President Doe. The second civil war (1999–2003) was fought between the newly-elected President Charles Taylor and several *other* warlords. The warlords also fought among themselves throughout the 14 years, creating a chaotic atmosphere in which no one was truly safe.

You may have heard of the civil war of Sierra Leone (the country founded by Great Britain for freed slaves) and the brutality associated with the trafficking in blood diamonds (diamonds traded to fund an invading army or warlord's activities). Liberia was not far behind in terms of atrocities. Just like in Sierra Leone, there were child soldiers, rapes, murders of civilians, looting, homes and villages burned, and many other horrors.

This period was quite unsettling, harsh, and challenging to the faith of Liberian Christians, but, as trials and suffering can do, it also drove many closer to God. At many times, it seemed there was no place to go and nobody but God to help Liberian Christians. Turning to God was a much better option than turning to alcohol or drugs and being filled with hate or vengeful violence to ease the pain. Unfortunately, some people did turn to alcohol or drugs!

As a Liberian, it is sad to think how long it took the international community to act. From 1996 to 2004, several attempts were made by the international community to broker peace and disarm the warlords. In 2003, the United Nations (UN) sent in thousands of troops to separate the warring factions and maintain peace. The warring factions were finally dissolved in November 2004.

A civil society resumed and elections were held. On November 23, 2005, the National Election Commission declared the American-educated Mrs. Ellen Johnson-Sirleaf the winner. When inaugurated on January 16, 2005, she was the first female President in Liberian history.

President Ellen Johnson-Sirleaf

At the Hague on April 26, 2012, Charles Taylor was convicted of war crimes for his involvement in the civil wars in Sierra Leone and Liberia. He was sentenced to 50 years in prison. Charles Taylor's son, Chuckie Taylor, was sentenced to prison in Florida for his role in crimes against humanity that occurred during the civil war.

# Esther Gbor's Story

Since so many died in the Liberian Civil War, it is easy to become numbed by the sheer weight of the numbers. Thus, let me share two stories of people I know.

The first story is about Esther Gbor, one of our first graduates of Liberian International Christian College (LICC). At the time of the civil war, she lived in the Ganta area. (She lives there again now.)

Geographically, the city of Ganta, Liberia, is close to Guinea. The border that separates the two countries is the St. John River. It is a large river during the rainy season. The St. John River Bridge that crosses this river is quite high—over 50 feet above the river at its highest point. It is also a narrow bridge—about one lane. Two cars cannot pass on the bridge.

When rebels attacked Ganta, the civilians fled, going in many different directions. Some fled into the surrounding countryside. However, most tried to flee across the bridge on foot. Fleeing into Guinea, a majority Muslim country, was a better option than staying, but it was not without its own dangers. As the massive crowds worked their way across the bridge, parents had to protect their children from falling into the river—even some adults fell into the river. Also, the children could easily have become confused and not even made it across the bridge before it was blocked. Fleeing such attacks was one of the worst times in the war. In the chaos that developed, family members and friends often became separated and many never found one another again! However, in spite of these risks, since the bridge was the only way to get out of Liberia and away from the rebels, people used it.

When I returned to Liberia in 2011, Pastors Dave Rodriquez and Keith Carlson from Grace Church in Noblesville, Indiana, and several United Liberia Inland Church Associates & Friends (ULICAF) Board members visited with us. On their second day, we travelled about a mile from LICC to the St. John River.

As we walked to the bridge, Esther told how the population of Ganta (around 30,000 people) had to flee when it was attacked simultaneously by an army of rebels and an army of mercenaries. Each group was fighting for control of Nimba County. Her husband was in school out of the country and she had to flee with six children, two of her own and four nieces and nephews. She turned and waved her arm across the rolling hills stretching from the north to the east and then to the south. She talked about how those hills were covered with a mass of humanity waiting to flee into Guinea when the border had closed that morning.

Guinea-Liberia Bridge over St. John River

Late that afternoon, Guinea opened the crossing, and everyone fled across. She said the discarded baggage was chest-deep across the valley. People tried to swim across the river, and many drowned. Her 17-year-old nephew carried her 4-year-old daughter on his back as he and three of the children swam across the river. They were rescued by Guineans who threw ropes to them and pulled them across.

Esther, who could not swim, had to cross the bridge with her baby on her back. She zig-zagged across the bridge with her head down and partially

11

covered because rebels walked among the crowd, shooting anyone they suspected of being sympathetic to the government. On the other side, she eventually found her children, and then they lived in a refugee camp for 6 months. Eventually, Esther's husband finished school and joined her. When they finally returned home, their house had been looted, the kitchen had been destroyed, and part of the tin roof had been stripped away. She was luckier than many whose houses had been burned to the ground. Now she is in the process of recovering and trying to rebuild her life. LICC has played a role in her recovery.

## Peter Nehsahn's Story

Many people lost their loved ones outright. For example, they were pulled out of line at checkpoints and summarily shot. Others did not know where their loved ones went. Many just disappeared.

My second story is about Dr. Peter Nehsahn, a man who has been a member of our ULICAF Board. His story exemplifies the second type of pain and grief that many Liberians experienced during the civil war. His pain is born from uncertainty.

It is a human quality to hope, even though we may be disappointed regularly. Realistically, in their hearts, people know that their loved ones are likely dead. But, if there is no body to bury, hope can be kept alive. Loved ones sometimes return.

In Peter's case, he will likely never know for certain what happened to his son. The best guess is his son was killed in the civil war, possibly while a member of one of the militias.

Peter's son may have experienced a parent's worst nightmare. Many children were forcibly recruited into one of the armies. Once there, they were forced to perpetrate the very violence that destroyed their *own* families!

His first trip back to Liberia to search for his son was in 2001. Liberia was not a safe place at that time and his search was hampered by the need to avoid endangering his family, or himself, or even his son. He left Liberia without meeting his son or knowing his whereabouts.

When he communicated with friends and family back in Liberia, he would ask about his son. Initially he would hear rumors that his son might have joined another militia or moved to a different county. As the years passed, bits of information became less frequent. Gradually, they faded completely.

When Peter returned in 2011, Liberia was a new nation. There was even a government bureau set up to help connect people who were separated by the war. He had no luck there, however.

And so Peter took to wandering the streets of Monrovia, finding places where young men gathered. He kept searching the faces for his son. He had not seen his son in 21 years. He knew his son would have matured and aged in that amount of time and he had aged some himself in 21 years. Yet, he hoped, as we all would, that there would be a miracle of God—either he would recognize his son or his son would recognize him.

He prayed that out of the thousands of people he passed on the street, one would be his son. He hoped that they would recognize each other. There was no news of his death, and so he could hope. That hope, as for so many others, was never realized. Where is his son? It's unknown to this day.

God answered many prayers for Peter, but He did not answer Peter's prayer to find his son on either his first or second trip to Liberia. We know that God will work good of all we give Him of our lives, but it is not always evident when the pain and loss is so great. (See Dr. Nehsahn's book *Someone Special Died at a Checkpoint in Liberia Today* available at *lulu.com* or for Nook on *barnesandnoble.com*.)

These are but a couple of stories that illustrate the horrors of the war. There are hundreds of thousands that could be told.

I can accurately say that all the current students at LICC are old enough to have experienced some of the horrors of war.

# Chapter 2:  Where We Started

## Keeping Hope Alive

Society in Liberia was not moving forward; instead, it was moving backwards at an alarmingly quick rate. People were not building; instead, there was destruction everywhere. When you walked down a street, you saw buildings pocked by bullet marks and roads littered with debris. People died because there were no health services.

As the situation further deteriorated, many of the wonderful relief services personnel from outside Liberia—missionaries, teachers, medical personnel, and other volunteers began to leave. Without their help, the situation grew even more desperate. Chaos and anarchy ruled. People hid in the bush for safety. At times, people were literally running for their lives. The civil war was a horrific conflict.

As Christians we are sustained by hope. We have faith that things can and will get better. No matter how grim it may seem in the midst of the battle, we believe that evil people with grim intentions will eventually fail. Sometimes they are overcome by good. Sometimes people are convicted of their evil intentions and abandon them because they clearly saw the suffering they caused others to endure. So hope is not wishful thinking that comes to fruition overnight, but it sometimes takes diligence effort before the dream is realized. We read in Proverbs: "Hope deferred makes the heart sick, but a longing fulfilled is a tree of life." (Prov. 13:12 NIV)

Working in Liberia while it was engulfed in civil war would have been difficult if not impossible. For those of us in America or other countries, it would have been difficult to do lasting good for Liberia while the war was ongoing. The Liberian refugee community in America needed to have optimism as we started. The most we could do was to help people survive a little longer. In a few cases, we could rescue them from that environment, but that would only be a *few* lucky people.

We could have looked at this seemingly hopeless situation and thought, "It will never get any better and will likely get even worse." With that attitude we probably would not have even started this long journey to healing of our nation. But we did hope and continued to pray and, eventually, the situation in Liberia began to change.

Eventually, the Liberian Civil War *did* come to an end. Our hope was realized. However, when we first started United Liberia Inland Church Associates & Friends (ULICAF) in America, the civil war was still raging in Liberia. We simply continued to place our hope in God and believe in our country and our countrymen.

Now, I want to make clear that I am not saying Liberia, as a country, was in a "perfect" condition prior to the civil war. We were in need of just about everything. We needed more improved roads, adequate hospitals, schools, more jobs, and definitely advanced technical training so workers could excel in their fields.

Also, I'm not saying it is a "perfect" country since the civil war ended. However, Liberian people are resilient. In spite of the horrors, we now have a civil society. Visitors and ex-pats who return see the visible changes in the country. If you drive or walk down a busy street in Monrovia, you witness a functioning society and a thriving marketplace. People are actively engaged in working to improve their lives. Though many will never be able to recover all that they lost due to the civil war, they are not defeated, lying down, and crying, nor are they any longer living in dread and fear for their lives. I've meandered down some streets in Monrovia, and thought, "Everyone is trying to create a business. Everyone is selling something. Since everyone is selling, who will be a buyer?"

The civil war left many people with absolutely nothing. But that does not matter. People are serious about moving forward. People are building new homes and sending their children to school. They believe in the power of education and want their children to have a better life than they had.

Liberia is no longer a society for lazy people. It is a country for those who want to build a new life and, in so doing, rebuild society.

Given that historical background, you now have some idea of what life was like in Liberia when we first started coming together to form what would eventually become United Liberia Inland Church Associates & Friends (ULICAF).

## Refugees Helping Refugees

The story of ULICAF starts with the diaspora. When Liberians first started arriving in America as refugees they had numerous immediate pressing needs. Many of those who arrived were from the war zone. They had few contacts, limited money, and the bare minimum of official papers. They were entering a new, strange culture that they did not understand.

In my case, I entered America in 1994 to pursue a Master's of Theology (ThM) at Western Theological Seminary in Holland, Michigan, followed by my wife Yah and our four children in 1995. It did not take long for Yah and me to start (maybe I should say restart) our ministry to Liberians. However, this time our community consisted of Liberian refugees and our mission field was to reach them wherever they lived in America.

We started to reach out to help Liberians. We initially did fundraising among my fellow theology students to raise funds to help a Liberian girl come to school in America.

In 1996, our family moved to Chicago, where many more Liberian refugees were arriving monthly and, sometimes, even weekly.

We continued our fundraising activity. Many who arrived did not know how to drive and, obviously, did not have driver's licenses. As you have probably guessed, cars were not that common in Liberia (in fact, they are still not that common in Liberia). Most families could not afford one. Almost everyone walked wherever they needed to go. In some locales in the U.S. a car is a necessity. It is the only practical way to get to a job or go to church, the grocery store, school, or a doctor. These new refugees needed to learn the most basic aspects of living in a city—like learning how to get a driver's license, buy a car, get insurance, and deal with a flat tire or an accident.

Some of the refugees who came over were like me. They had some education and language skills. Many, however, were low in skills and did not have much education. Some were unable to fill out basic job applications. Since they did not know enough English, we helped them.

Once refugees had been here a while, they learned how to navigate better through the culture (or at least they knew more than the very new arrivals), so we could more effectively help each other. As these self-help communities developed, the Christians among us (most of the refugees were raised Christians or had since converted to Christianity) began fellowshipping in small groups. The Liberian Christian refugee community bonded together in these meetings. Most of us did not have our own Liberian churches (and still do not today). Instead, we gathered in small house groups. The groups would meet weekly or maybe every couple of weeks. We shared food or coffee and talked about our experience during the civil war and our new life as refugees in America.

The fellowship groups were important to us as refugees for building morale and gaining emotional and practical support. However, these gatherings were just as important, or even more important, to our Christian faith. Everyone had experienced some level of disruption and trauma. These types of experiences can bring a believer closer to God—or they can cause a believer to question his/her faith. We were dealing with serious theological questions like, "How could a good God allow horrors like those of the Liberian Civil War?" and "Why was I saved from death, but not my friends and relatives?"

As a pastor, I was concerned about more than just my own personal faith and that of my family. Along with other pastors and elders among the Liberian refugee community, I was concerned about our *community*. There are ready answers to these tough questions, but answers like "God gives us freewill and some people abuse it" or "God saved you for a purpose—He wants to fulfill a plan for your life" are also traditional answers Christian give. However, these answers did not satisfy most of us; the reality of a living faith necessitated that we all had to personally find answers for ourselves in our own situations. In our fellowship groups we had the opportunity to process our experiences and help each other find healing.

Meanwhile, we received letters from Liberian refugees still in Liberia or in other countries. They wanted us to sponsor them to come to America. As a community, we did what we could, but we quickly exhausted the means we had available to offer affidavits of support. So, we increasingly reached out to the larger American community. This became more regular and was a blessing as we started "partnerships" with our new American Christian friends.

The growth of these small Christian refugee fellowship groups is something I can talk about from my own personal experience. The growth of these Christian fellowship groups was expanding into most of the Liberian communities across America. This was not in just one state or one particular region. We were coming together everywhere. Soon we had groups in Chicago, Minneapolis, Atlanta, Philadelphia, and in 2002, a group was established in Indianapolis when my wife Yah and I (and our children) moved there.

## Coming Together as ULICAF

There were many needs in Liberia—many, many needs! We were a refugee people—a people with resources, but limited ones. We could not solve all the worlds' problems, or even all of Liberia's crippling problems, so we knew we needed to narrow our focus. It was during this time that we developed some core guiding principles. We were Liberians for Liberia. We did not want to rely solely on others. As we talked, we began to grow our faith. We began to believe: "We can do this." We began to believe we were going to be part of the solution. We began to share this dream among ourselves. A man or woman can build his or her own vision of the future by focusing on good and working to achieve it. So much more can be accomplished when two or more people band together to build each other's faith. Confidence grows even deeper among a covenant community that is committed to a cause. By sharing with each other we began to believe in our vision and in ourselves.

We wanted to do more than help each other here in America and a few friends or family in Liberia. Our vision was for Liberian refugees to come together to make an impact on all those who remained behind in Liberia and Liberia as a nation. One of the issues we had to deal with as we came together in large gatherings was maintaining cooperation. It would not accomplish our goals to just increase in numbers if we could not work together. We needed a structure that engaged as many of our members as possible. This meant having an organization that would both *respect* the individuality of all the members while maintaining a vision that would also *engage* all of our members.

Let me give you an example of what I mean. When I tell this, some people laugh, but the person who told me this story was quite serious. I talked to someone from the East coast about our organization of Liberian refugees. He responded to me, "You are getting Liberians to cooperate? How is that possible?" He then went on to tell the story of soccer leagues in his city. Many different groups had teams. However, the Liberians always struggled to field a team. He said that this happened because the players and coaches could not come to an agreement on their strategies, and as a consequence, kept splintering into smaller groups. The Liberians he knew could not seem to put aside their differences to ever cooperate as a team.

We laid aside our own independence, pride, and plans (which could have separated us). I believe it was our faith in God and seeking His will together that kept us together. We focused on the ideas we could do to really help our country. Eventually we established a clear vision for the organization. I would share our vision at every opportunity that I had to talk to my countrymen. We had few leadership conflicts and few people left our fellowship. When we did have disagreements, most of them were not with the vision, but *how* to best accomplish the vision.

## ULICAF Receives Non-Profit Status

Since very few of our leaders had served in leadership positions in an organization, we learned as we went along. That did not stop us from moving forward. We came together with a hope and with a depth of character that comes from surviving great trials. We knew Christ; we had faith; we believed that even though we were a scattered people, God could bring us together. We worked to learn the things we needed to know to start an organization. When we did not have the answers, we looked for those who did.

Initially Grace Church in Noblesville, Indiana, helped us by receiving and processing our contributions through their in-house missionary fund. However, Grace was advised to change their administrative policy when working with and assisting non-American citizens and their ministries, so they could no longer receive gifts and then pay them out to us. We were forced to be totally independent as we continued to develop and grow our ministry.

One of my prayer friends strongly encouraged us to start our own 501(c)(3) non-profit organization. More importantly, Attorney Jeffrey Adams patiently walked us through the whole process. When we started, I knew absolutely nothing about even the first steps of filing for a tax-exempt status. Attorney Adams, however, was an expert and had helped set up many of these types of organizations. He helped us register ULICAF with the State of Indiana as a non-profit. He then helped us apply for an Employer Identification Number (EIN) for ULICAF and prepared the IRS Form 1023, *Application for Recognition of Exemption*, which the Federal IRS uses to determine tax status. This form is over 20 pages long! Even more difficult was that the IRS processing office insisted that we prove that our international partnership in Liberia was genuine and in the interest of humanitarian service.

Being 501(c)(3) means that our organization has been approved by the Internal Revenue Services as tax-exempt, with the following purposes: charitable, religious, and educational. As my American readers will know, as a non-profit organization, people can donate money to us and it is tax deductible for them. The organization does not have to pay tax on the money because we are using the money for charitable causes that the U.S. Government acknowledges will positively change lives. After several months of going back and forth and incurring higher costs, it was a day of celebration when we achieved non-profit status. It meant we could now legally operate in America as a non-profit and receive gifts from donors all over the country.

# Chapter 3: The Vision of ULICAF

## Identifying the Need

One of the first challenges we had was to agree on a goal. We knew we wanted to help Liberia, but where should we start? What would be our passion, our main focus? Over time, and after many long meetings, we reached a consensus. We realized that quality education and training was one of the biggest and most immediate needs of Liberia and would impact Liberia's future in many ways.

The civil war had devastating effects on Liberia, but the loss of educated people would affect its future in myriad ways. Most of the educated professional people had fled the strife or were dead. Liberia needed its own skilled people in many fields and industries to begin and continue the road to recovery. They could not just depend upon outside relief from other countries.

We asked ourselves the question, "Would anyone want to go to a hospital that had no doctor?" And having our own Liberian doctors would build confidence and pride again in the leaders of the local communities. We began to see how that applied to many professions and industries.

Our roads were in disrepair. Why? Not only were resources limited to improve the roads, but there was a severe lack of skilled engineers as well as a lack of construction workers knowledgeable in building roads. We could one day have great hospitals, but unless we have roads to get people there, they still would not get the care they needed.

We also needed people who were skilled in designing and building houses. In Liberia, the houses built today follow the same dated design as those built in the 1960s. In Liberia we do not have very many architects to design new and better house plans that are suited for our culture and environment. It gets extremely hot in Liberia and we experience heavy downpours in our rainy season. We definitely needed more architects to face the growing needs of a developing country.

## The Importance of Education

In Liberia, we struggle to give quality training to enough people to adequately serve our community. Our vision was to offer quality education in a number of areas—business leadership and accounting, Bible and theology (to train future pastors and ministry leaders), agri-business with new farming techniques, education to provide trained teachers, and nursing. In God's kingdom, we encourage our people, whether they are educated or not, to love and serve others even when there is no reward monetarily. But, without the skills and knowledge gained through education and work experience, we have little to give *practically* to our people. So we viewed our vision of providing quality education as extremely essential for not only one's personal development to provide for his or her own family, but as a way to impact the whole nation of Liberia.

Education changes people and, thus, all of society. What do I mean by that? For example, consider the suffering caused by the brutality and violence of war. Educated people are less likely to choose violence as a solution to their personal or national problems. They will pursue other options of change. They will be less likely to blame leaders or to believe the society has abandoned them. If they have a stake in society by operating a small business and they are productively using their time, they will want to be part of the solution by helping their community. They will not want to engage in violence and the destruction of property; they will find new meaning and value in their work and they will respect other people's property and lives.

If a Liberian has the responsibility of caring for children and maintaining a house, he will be focused on working to pay the mortgage. With a good education one can then envision a future for himself—a life not limited by the hourly minimum wage. I'll give you a good example.

One ULICAF member who came to America as a child refugee was sponsored by a woman to attend a university in Indianapolis. He studied and applied himself and was obviously very thankful for this wonderful opportunity. It took him many years of effort to eventually become a dentist. Now he has even more to give back. In December 2011, he and his wife gave $20,000 to help rebuild churches in Liberia and $25,000 to build LICC. It was a quality education that enabled him to give $45,000, but it was his Christian Biblical values that helped him choose ULICAF and LICC.

Not every Liberian has the money or opportunity or connections to come to America. We need to provide education for the people there. Working 2, and at times 3 jobs to survive, they are willing to make the sacrifices to obtain a good education. But who will build these schools? The government has limited resources as they recover from the civil war. That is why we believe God has blessed LICC at this time in Liberia's development as a nation. And we are a *Christian* witness to the whole country!

## Value–Based Education

We have seen that an education pursued without character development often leads to personal greed. For ULICAF, education is not just about *knowledge*. We believe the best education needs to be based on values for the greatest good of all society.

People with Christian values give back to their family, their friends, their community, and their nation. The refugees who started ULICAF have all in one way or another given back to Liberia and impacted lives. They are not wealthy people; many of our founding members were factory workers, laborers, restaurant workers, and janitors. Yet, they took from their very limited resources, thanking God for whatever financial blessings they had—large or small—and gave sacrificially to the cause. They started giving immediately, practicing the discipline of giving from whatever they had, even if it was little. They were like the widow (in the story told by Jesus) who contributed her last mite to help fulfill God's plan:

> *Jesus sat down opposite the place where the offerings were put and watched the crowd putting their money into the temple treasury. Many rich people threw in large amounts. But a poor widow came and put in two very small copper coins, worth only a few cents. Calling his disciples to him, Jesus said, "Truly I tell you, this poor widow has put more into the treasury than all the others. They all gave out of their wealth; but she, out of her poverty, put in everything—all she had to live on."* Mark 12:41-44 (NIV)

A value-based education enhances society in two ways. First, the educated person is able to personally prosper and contribute economically. Second, the educated person with character is more likely to make the sacrifices needed to help the community. We have witnessed this repeatedly among the members of ULICAF.

## What Type of Education?

We next considered the many different ways we could help educate Liberians. One of the ways we could do this was to sponsor students to come to America and attend a university like the Liberian refugee who became a dentist. And we did do this in a few cases, but we realized that only one in a thousand could benefit from this method. If our goal was to impact Liberia we also knew that many of those who received an education in America would end up staying there. The Liberians who became nurses in America could take short-term medical mission trips to Liberia, but the effect would be short-lived.

On the other hand we recognized some positive effects of Liberians *staying* in America. Like many immigrants in America representing many other cultures and nations, working American Liberians would send back money to help their struggling families and friends. A substantial portion of the grass-roots development in Liberia is accomplished this way. Liberian refugees send money home to help family members with day-to-day living, to educate family members, to repair existing houses or help build new ones, to provide capital for small businesses, and to support the local church. The benefit is not only in terms of the immediate physical help that money obviously brings, but also in the hope it raises. The many Liberian refugees who live in the developed world have seen hope. They understand that investing in the future can and does pay off and they are able to share that hope with the Liberians they know. The bottom line, though, is that the Liberian society needs widespread education right there in the communities of Liberia.

Even before I left Africa to study in America back in 1994, I talked with friends about this. Many educated Liberians encouraged me and understood that educated leaders would be the backbone of the country when civil society was restored.

There were many types of education that Liberia needed. Some education is very basic; the foundations of reading, writing, and math are essential. The Liberian government is working to address these basic needs. Even in a developing nation many can rely on cell phones, radio, and TV; however, reading is the initial pathway to successful employment. We knew that the government was focused on providing those basic educational needs. The biggest challenge for a developing country, from our perspective, was to provide college education.

If children are to learn to read and write and to do basic math, someone has to teach them. If a student decides to continue their schooling beyond high school, someone needs to teach them in that setting as well. We decided we would help fill that gap with the creation of Liberian International Christian College (LICC). We could provide an opportunity for large numbers of Liberian students to pursue higher education. We could help hundreds who would not otherwise be able to receive an education.

## Balancing Education and Values

At one of the colleges I attended, the focus of the education was only on the Bible. My goal was to be a better trained minister and it did effectively prepare me for future ministry. Most students, however, want a broader based education. A degree in "Biblical Studies" would be helpful if they want to be a minister. But if they are looking for non-ministerial work, they need skills, experiences, and training in a specific job or vocation. The biblical values and ethics they learned at the Bible College would be applied to make them trustworthy and diligent workers in their future career. The problem is that they desperately need specific training in secular work!

For example, a future farmer does not need four years of theology. Instead, he needs a basic grounding in God's Word and a complete knowledge of how to grow food for his community. But, that was not the model we witnessed in our Liberian community. Some other African countries operate in much the same manner. I went to a wonderful Bible college in Nairobi and was trained to become a better pastor. I got a Divinity Degree. While that type of training would have been a wonderful experience for a farmer, what he really needed to be a better farmer were courses in soil science, crop management, pest control, and basic accounting.

If your gift and calling is to be a minister of the gospel, then studying the Bible for four years can adequately prepare you. However, not everyone is called to full-time ministry. So, ULICAF did not want to limit its focus on building a Bible college. We wanted a college with a broader curriculum which was founded on God's Word. We wanted a college that would infuse its students with a knowledge of God and of His Word, a concern for His church, and the desire to spread the Good News. We wanted a college that would achieve a balance between professional training and biblical knowledge. We also wanted a college that would allow students to enter a variety of professions.

## A Broader Curriculum

We wanted to produce well-rounded students. Over the course of a person's career, a well-rounded person will have more opportunities than someone who simply is educated for one specific career. If we want students to achieve their full potential—for themselves and for society—it was important for them to know the rudiments of the social sciences, math, and economics, how society functions.

Let's look at the study of psychology. All pastors are counselors that give advice to their church people all the time. And it obviously should be *biblically-based* counseling, since the Bible provides everything a person needs to solve any personal problem. But a pastor is limited to reaching specific people within his sphere of influence in the church. Christians who are educated for many different job opportunities will go into the marketplace and directly influence those around him.

Most students who take psychology classes will not end up being professional psychologists. That is okay now in Liberia, because while there are many in-depth counseling needs due to the trauma of the war, there are not many job openings for psychologists. But trained lay "biblical counselors" can apply what they have learned in all the interpersonal challenges they face at work. Workers with personal problems will soon find that the Christian who is trained at LICC is not only a compassionate person but one who is skilled and has wisdom to help another work through a problem. This is why we believe that a liberal arts Christian college and the benefits of such a diverse education can impact every area of the marketplace in Liberia. Also, while the students are living in the LICC community, they will have plenty of opportunity to apply the biblical knowledge they have learned to real-life situations. The students will learn to biblically "counsel" one another.

The prior model for missionary funding of colleges was to provide a *free* education to almost all the students. LICC, however, developed a different philosophy. We wanted LICC to be accessible and affordable to all, but *not* free to all students. We strongly believed this model would develop *ownership* in our students. People place more value on education that requires at least some sacrifice.

# Chapter 4:  Why This Type

# of School

When I published my first book, *No More War*, LICC was half of a building on a plot of land outside Ganta with a few students scheduled to start classes. We had a dream, one that we felt very much was in God's will, but we were a long way from finishing it. We knew the beginning, but we did not know the middle or end of the story. As I write and publish this book, LICC is a fully accredited college. We have now graduated several classes and expect continued growth for many years to come. We can now see the culmination of our dream. We have successfully built a school, with God's help, dedicated to developing Godly leaders.

First Building: Half-finished but Usable in 2009

First Building: Finished, with Faculty

So, if the first book was about the "what" of our dream, this book is about the "how." Before we get into the story of "how," I would like to tell a story that illustrates "why" we were motivated to do this work for God. It is from an interview with one our graduates, Pastor E. Simon Miaway.

Simon grew up in Gampa Village in Nimba County. His father was a polygamist with lots of children. His father could not afford to educate them. Simon slowly drifted away from God, but returned to the Lord through a crusade in his hometown after the death of his father. Following his conversion, he became active in the church his mother headed in his village, and eventually attended Monrovia Bible Institute. Because of the civil war, he returned to Nimba County where he married and helped plant 4 churches in Gbehyi. In 2004 he moved to the city of Ganta to raise his 5 children.

In Pastor Miaway's own words:

> I was very excited when I learnt about the plans to establish LICC in Ganta. We started work at the proposed college site for two years before ULICAF decided to build the school. I was among the first batch of candidates to sit for the entrance exam, and I was successful.
>
> Being a student at LICC was a tremendous blessing for me; as an Evangelist, my focus was meeting new people and preaching salvation to them. LICC improved my skills and made me a better pastor, teacher, and counselor; I can now preach to people, and can equally train others to preach. My favorite subject was English Language; because I was denied education when I was young, I was very weak in English and lacked the confidence for public speaking. But all this changed when I came to LICC. Before LICC, I was somewhat limited in reading and interpreting the Bible, and preparing sermons. LICC disclosed the secret to me.

*I encourage two or more people to enroll at the school every semester. LICC is [God's gift] to the people of Nimba County and beyond; it is within easy reach, and affordable.*

Presently Simon is Assistant Pastor of the United Liberia Inland Church in Ganta. This is the type of life transformation we were hoping to effect by providing an opportunity for more Liberians to receive a quality education.

# Chapter 5: The Leadership
# of ULICAF

## The ULICAF Board of Directors

To create ULICAF as a non-profit organization, we were legally required to have a Board of Directors. We could no longer continue to make decisions on our own, but were required by law to have at least a president, a secretary, and a treasurer.

ULICAF has supporters reaching beyond Indiana since Liberians live across the country, giving us a national board. We have two current members from Georgia; two from Florida; four from Minnesota; three from Illinois; and three from Indiana.

Once a year we get together, usually in November, to review what we have accomplished during the year. We discuss our current programs, and carefully evaluate the work of both the organization and the Board itself. It is during this annual board meeting that we set our goals for the following year and discuss the needs for student scholarships. We also have a wonderful time of prayer and fellowship. These board meetings have helped all of us get to personally know and love each other as brothers and sisters in Christ.

The rest of the year, we meet once a month on a telephone conference call. We also meet if an issue comes up that needs to be addressed in a short time frame. We consider these meetings quite important and value the input of all the members.

We always ask existing Board members for recommendations for additional or replacement board members and advisors. Also, if a Board member no longer wants to be active, we ask them if they know anybody who they believe has a passion for our type of ministry and who can join us in leading ULICAF.

For elections, a Nominations Committee recommends a slate of candidates for open positions who would serve for a term of 3 years. The whole board then votes on these nominations. If a Board member is active and passionate about our mission, of course, we would like them to stay for a second term or even longer.

Like most boards, we use a series of committees to oversee the day-to-day operations of the organization. Almost all board members are on at least one committee and many are on multiple committees.

## Finance Committee

This committee is responsible for the approval of funding, financial oversight of our activities, and reviewing our financial statements. For approving day-to-day expenses, we operate through a tiered approach which gives us flexibility and accountability. For example, the Executive Director can approve expenditures from $1 to $499 without consulting with other Finance Committee members. For $499 to $2,000 expenditures, the Finance Committee must give approval. For sums that are higher than $2,000, the decision is taken to the full Board for approval. As an example, an individual can approve office supplies and other small expenses; the Finance Committee can approve the purchase of small equipment and facilitating our programs, but the *whole* Board must approve a new building and all transfers of funds toward specific projects.

## Program Committee

One of the primary responsibilities of this committee is to screen potential partner organizations. Our goal is to find organizations with strategic goals that are aligned with the work of ULICAF and then partner with them to accomplish shared goals.

When we receive a letter from a prospective new partner organization, this committee evaluates the potential for an ongoing beneficial relationship between ULICAF/ LICC and this person or organization. We follow a carefully structured process and "checklist" of items needed to make an informed decision as to whether to proceed. If we decide to move forward, the committee writes a Memorandum of Understanding.

This committee also develops and maintains our online presence. Russ Schwartz manages our website (www.ulicaf.org) and Miss Neplenser Wahkeleh, a volunteer in Florida, manages our Facebook® page. Very early on we realized that ULICAF could provide efficient, high quality services and expert ministry teams only if we use a "partnership" model.

## Planning Committee

These individuals work most of the year planning and preparing for our annual meeting. They find a host location and develop a local city committee to support and organize various activities. The Annual Meeting includes a dinner with a special speaker and music. This dinner is also a major fundraiser. The keynote speaker gives a motivational message that serves both as an exhortation to maintain the vision of the ministry and as method of sharing the financial needs to fulfill the next steps in the vision.

## Communications Committee

The primary responsibility of this committee is our quarterly newsletter. It is our main means of communicating with our members, donors and *potential* donors. Through this important communication piece, we are able to update our friends of the ministry about exciting accomplishments and our goals for the future. Newsletters are available on our website (www.ulicaf.org).

## Fundraising Committee

We have been blessed by so many faithful donors that sacrificially give to enable us to fulfill our ministry calling to the nation of Liberia. Another avenue that we have used to expand the ministry has been applying for larger grants. We have successfully appealed to Christian foundations in this country. We have also been blessed by commitments made by the Liberian government to LICC because of our commitment to provide quality education to Liberians. This committee is led by the Executive Director who meets directly with various pastors, directors of mission committees, university directors, and foundation directors, to share the vision, goals, and needs of ULICAF/LICC. The Executive Director also assists in writing these grants.

## Executive Committee

This committee, comprised of the President, Vice-President, Secretary, and Treasurer focuses on leadership challenges and official public communications. The Executive Committee acts as the "voice" of ULICAF. Before we publish major communications, the Executive Committee reviews them to ensure that they are consistent with our policy. All major organizations face leadership and communications challenges. ULICAF is no different and must deal biblically with conflict as it arises. The New Testament addresses conflict head-on:

> *If your brother sins against you, go and show him his fault, just between the two of you. If he listens to you, you have won your brother over. But if he will not listen, take one or two others along, so that every matter may be established by the testimony of two or three witnesses.* Matthew 18:15-16 (NIV)

We have been blessed in that we have not had to deal with major relationship conflicts in ULICAF. If, for example, a board member misses several meetings or neglects clear responsibilities, the Executive Committee shares their concern with that specific member. We do not want to potentially embarrass or shame any member, but want to love them and exhort them as Jesus would have us do.

Obviously, there are often reasonable (and hopefully temporary) conflicts of schedule and family or medical problems that keep our members from attending these meetings. We want our board members to have an excitement about their responsibilities. Unfortunately, specific outside issues might require an individual board member to resign.

## ULICAF Presidents

Although I am the co-founder and President of LICC and Executive Director of ULICAF, I am not the President of the ULICAF Board. The Board President is a separate position. Our first Board President (2003 to 2007) was Karney Dunah. He was a great leader who demonstrated faithfulness to God; I could always count on him to lead our board meetings by speaking the truth. He also spoke into my life timely, powerful words that I needed. He worked diligently to build relationships within our organization. As a result, we became more than co-workers.

Since 2007 we have had other presidents. They varied in both background and management style, but each one effectively worked to rally people, build unity, and refine vision to keep it fresh in our minds.

Left to right: Dr. Shadrach Gonqueh, Jeanette Edgecomb, Dr. Peter and Julie Nehsahn, Karney and Lydia Dunah, Matthew Sakeuh, Mark Dhan, Helen Dahn, Romeo and Pauline Dahn, Paul and Mercy Miantona and Yah and Sei Buor

Our second President was Shadrach Gonqueh. Shadrach came to America as a refugee during the Liberian diaspora. He went to college at the University of Indianapolis, a Methodist college. He then went on to Dental School at Indiana University in downtown Indianapolis. He was our Board President for almost two years. Shadrach, with his strong organizational skills, enabled the Board to fulfill various ministry commitments. He was very straightforward with all of us. However, when he started his own dental practice, he was unable to continue as Board President due to his increased workload. Although Shadrach stepped down, he continues to support ULICAF financially as well as with any time his schedule allows.

As of this writing, our Board President is Paul Miantona. Paul is one of the youngest of our group. He and his wife Marcy, a nurse, live in

Minneapolis. Paul started his Board Presidency in 2012 and communicates passionately what LICC is doing in Liberia. He has also brought a youthful vision and creativity to the ministry. Paul is a businessman by training and profession and has an undergraduate degree in Computer Information Systems and a MBA in Finance from the Keller Graduate School of Management. He works for Wells Fargo in Minnesota.

Though younger than most (but not all) of our Board members, he shares the experience of the Liberian diaspora. He came to America through the sponsorship of Lutheran World Service. He had struggled to survive as one of the 80,000 Liberian refugees in the Danane Refugee camp in the Ivory Coast. In Paul's own words,

> *Life in the refugee camp in Danane was very challenging and inhumane. I remember the only solution to constant worrying, hunger, and thirst was sleeping! As refugees, we also faced discrimination because the Ivory Coast economy was threatened because of the non-stop influx of Liberians. Thousands of Liberians were perceived as destabilizing the Ivorian economy. On occasion, I found myself homeless, but I trusted God to be in control of my life, and eventually my housing situation stabilized and I was able to enroll in a refugee high school. It was at this time that I realized that in order to change my current situation and become successful, I needed to focus on my education and excel in it.*

Once in America, Paul began a humble work career at a Wendy's restaurant. As he continued to focus on his education, God answered his prayers by providing the opportunity to enroll in Trinity Christian College in Palos Heights, Illinois. In 2000, Paul joined with other Liberians to start ULICAF. Paul, though he had limited time in his schedule, was always willing to volunteer. As a consequence, he developed his leadership abilities and took on increasingly greater responsibility with ULICAF. We are proud to have helped mentor him for leadership and look forward to his work mentoring others.

2013 ULICAF Board Members

Board Members in the photo: Back row: Wesley Lankah, Illinois; Yah Buor, Indiana; Dr. Sei Buor, Executive Director, Indiana; Lydiah Dunah, Illinois; Karney Dunah, Assistant Executive Director, Illinois; Ruby Gonqueh, Indiana; Dr. Shadrach Gonqueh Past President, Indiana. Front row: Mercy Lankah, Illinois; Jim Tremblay, Indiana; Jeanette Edgecomb, Florida; Nicole Conrad, Indiana; Ruth Schwartz, Treasurer, Indiana; Lydia Wahkeleh, Florida; Foster Wahkeleh, Florida; and Glen Gbakoyah, Secretary, Minnesota.

The 2013 ULICAF Board members not in the picture: Paul Miantona, Minnesota, President; Mark Dahn, Vice President, Florida; Chris Luogon, Minnesota; Peter Nehsahn, Georgia; Chris Scott, Illinois; and Narko Wuanti, Minnesota.

## Formation of the Advisory Board

In the spring of 2013, the ULICAF Board realized that LICC had grown to such a point that it needed to restructure its organizational leadership. Membership levels had been flat for the past 5 years and we had run out of new contacts. During the summer and fall of 2013, ULICAF recruited, oriented, and launched its first Advisory Board. The 17 members of the Advisory Board assist the ULICAF Executive Director. These new "advisors" brought with them not only financial resources, but knowledge in many areas of business—planning, agriculture, computers, and architectural design. They are true ambassadors for ULICAF. Generally, each member interacts with and provides advice to the Executive Director or other governing Board members about 3 to 4 times a year as needed by ULICAF. This Advisory Board communicates the ULICAF core message to their contacts and invites them to also participate in ULICAF.

As of 2015, our Advisory board includes: Mr. Jim Berndt, Ms. Karen Bodach, Mr. Danny Bowen, Mr. Donald Cassel, Mr. Ed Fischer, Mr. Howard Foreman, Mr. Ralph Forey, Mr. Tom Green, Mr. Chuck Gross, Ms. Polly Harrington, Retired Colonel Randy Johnson, Mr. John Jurgenson, Mr. John Lieberman, Mr. Byron Miller, Mr. Russ Schwartz, Mr. Paul Thompson, and Mr. John Wright.

## Leading ULICAF and LICC

Once we had established a clear vision of helping Liberia through the building of a college, we needed someone to lead the effort. That person turned out to be me. I was a pastor and a leader with organizational leadership training (that was the area of my doctorate), but I did not yet know how being such a leader would look.

As the co-founder and President of LICC, I faced a daunting task. None of us ever had experienced being a leader of a high school or college. We knew that we were embarking on a venture that far exceeded training a few teachers and supporting a grade school in one of the rural counties. That work is truly important, of course, but it is something we could have done with relative ease. We knew that this grander vision would be challenging and would require the focused dedication of myriad people for many years.

Where should we start? There were so many things to consider. Where would the students come from? What would our curriculum look like? Where would we build the school, and where would we get an architect to design it? How would we get accreditation? And practically, where would the money come from?

So this was a new experience for ULICAF. This was also a new experience for me. As the leaders of ULICAF, we struggled to get a clear vision of all that was involved to actually build a sustainable college to educate Liberians for Christ. I also personally struggled with figuring out and prioritizing what I needed to do as an individual leader of this project.

Eventually, I was able to narrow it down to one very important question, "As a leader, what do *I* need to contribute to get this vision off the ground?" I had to assess realistically my own skills and experience. Did I have what it takes? My wife can tell you that I spent a number of sleepless nights as I pondered and analyzed what I needed to do. I knew that I had an ability as a teacher, but I was not skilled in all the academic areas needed for the curriculum for a Christian liberal arts college.

I'm fairly efficient using a personal computer, but did not know anything about setting up a website or teaching others about using computers. I can balance our family checkbook, but I was not an accountant. Someone needed to keep the books. I had limited finances to contribute financially. When it came time to construct a building, I had some ability to make a few bricks, but it would not be nearly enough to build a school! Thus, I needed to put together a construction team.

In those beginning months I was totally dependent on God and many faithful friends who helped me think through all that I needed to do get this project started and manage all the aspects of it.

## Leadership Qualities

I wanted to have fellow co-leaders to come alongside me, affirming my calling to lead this venture and helping in the leadership, so I set up an election process for *all* our leaders. This included even who the future Executive Director/President would be. I wanted to know that my fellow Liberians wanted me to lead them in this awesome vision and great responsibility. And I wanted to be sure that we would be seeking God for our future leaders. I knew I could not do this tremendous job indefinitely and must plan for succession.

When I was elected as the first President of ULICAF, I realized everyone bought into the vision I had and also believed I had the ability, skill, and education to articulate that vision to others.

I believe my fellow Liberians saw my faithfulness and that if I committed to something or said I would do something, I would work diligently to make it happen. I wanted to be able to go to people and say, "This is what I said I would do and this is what I did." I also believe our ULICAF members realized that if the truth needed to be spoken on any issue, I would be honest with them and share it.

Because of my prior connections and experience in Liberia, many of these former refugees who supported me were elementary and high school students I had taught. I had their respect and confidence. When they came to America, they trusted my leadership which made it easier for them to embrace and support me in my new leadership role as founding President of LICC.

The Board recognized my commitment to Christian unity. Division or disunity among the various tribal groups is not only a problem in Liberia, but also in the United States. They believed that I could bring a much-needed unity among the various Christian groups and overcome the real differences that drove a wedge between us during the civil war.

Why would God choose me?

I have asked that question many times. I was not raised in a Christian home while many of my peers are not only second generation believers, but some are third generation Christians! I have faith that I will see my mother in heaven, but I do not know if my father was converted before he died. So why would God choose someone who did not have a long Christian legacy of godly Christian family members?

We all see through a glass, darkly, today in this present world. One day we will be with Him and then we will see God's plan clearly. But I think that God saw, given my humble beginnings, that I as a first generation believer (without even a single believer in my village), would give God all the credit for anything significant that would be accomplished for His kingdom. If I achieved anything, it was not the result of my grandfather's faith or my mother's faith, or anyone else's faith; it would be the result of the combined faith of the ULICAF community!

I think God saw my commitment to keep my word. Early on in my Christian life, when the missionaries decided to retire and go back home, I went to God in prayer. I prayed, "God, I want to do what the missionaries are doing, but I do not have the required training and skills to minister effectively to others. I do not understand the Bible well. I am afraid that I will fail miserably if I try. However, God, if you help me, I will step out and follow you like these missionaries did." God saw that I wanted to serve Him and he answered those prayers. Eventually, God did provide opportunities to further my education. I diligently studied the Bible and as I learned more about ways to evangelize my people, I went out and shared what I had learned with my community. I was blessed as many in my immediate family were among those who came to a saving knowledge of Jesus through my witness to them.

## Commitment to the Vision

Personally, nothing in my professional life is more important than pursuing the vision of LICC. We started with a lot of passion and excitement and almost everyone we talked with encouraged us. But I also knew that I needed to get many others onboard in practical ways or it would just be a "dream." So what was the basic plan we developed to put feet to our prayers?

# Chapter 6: The Basic Plan and the Foundation

## The Three Corded Rope (Ecclesiastes 4:12)

As the board wrestled with how we could better communicate this vision of building a college, we came up with the biblical text:

> *Though one may be overpowered, two can defend themselves. A cord of three strands is not quickly broken.* Ecclesiastes 4:12 (NIV)

Thus, our "three-corded rope" to build an institution dedicated to (1) community, (2) learning, and (3) worship is built on the perfect Trinity: Father, Son, and the Holy Spirit. We summarized it as knowledge of the Father, service to the Son, and being led by faith by the Holy Spirit.

The *first* cord of the rope is **Knowledge** represented by the **pursuit of academic excellence**. Through critical inquiry and research we wanted to encourage a balanced total understanding of our culture and the world. We envisioned a building with 18 classrooms that would provide an environment for research in the areas of business, education, technology, nursing, agriculture, leadership and other practical areas that would equip Liberians in the workplace. We also hoped to provide a place for the local Ganta community to learn. For this reason we wanted a library and medical clinic that could benefit the community.

The *second* cord of the rope is **Service** focused on **equipping our students to serve Christ across the nation of Liberia**. Service referred to the wide range of activities designed to meet the needs (outside of the school classroom environment) and *within the local community.* We wanted to provide participating students a good working knowledge on many subjects as well as a foundation in biblical ethics.

The *third* cord of the rope is **Faith**. We are a **worshipping and learning community**. Chapel is mandatory for our staff, faculty, and students from Monday through Thursday. When a physical chapel is constructed, it will serve as the place for students and the local community to worship God together.

This 3-corded enduring vision for the college helped us keep our focus on both the students and the community.

## The Campus Master Plan and Strategic Planning Meetings

I needed a detailed plan and a drawing of what this college might look like. But I did not know any architects and did not have the money to hire one. But God had a plan.

After I graduated from Loyola University, we were unable to return home to start LICC because of the civil war. Instead, we moved to Noblesville, Indiana. We were looking for a rental house and we learned that a Christian couple, Ruth and Russ Schwartz, had a cottage in the back of their property that they rented at a nominal cost to people in ministry who were in transition. In our case, we were waiting for the civil war in Liberia to end so that we could return home.

When I met him, I did not know of Russ's history or his love of architecture. One day I saw him constructing a patio on the back of his house. He had personally designed it; I witnessed his passion for this project. I felt inspired to discuss our plans for LICC with him. The patio beautifully restored the outward appearance of the house giving it a turn-of-the-century look. One Wednesday evening, I asked Russ to have some coffee with me. I wanted to talk to him about this patio and how he knew so much about architectural design.

I already knew that Russ worked in information technology. He told me about his childhood passion and how he had designed and constructed a variety of buildings such as a service station and a Gothic cathedral all out of cardboard or paper. He told me that one time he built a city using paper streets taped to the linoleum floor and used cardboard boxes for buildings. He went on to say that in his teens he studied drafting and designed a whole line of cars for an imaginary car company. He then went on to compete in architectural design competitions.

Given this passion in the field of architecture at a young age, it was no surprise that he majored in architectural drafting in high school in hopes of becoming an architect. However, he was concerned about the overdevelopment he saw around him in his hometown in Ohio. Although he never realized that goal of becoming an architect, he still maintained a life-long interest in design. Eventually, his interest in architecture was rekindled when he read Christopher Alexander's book, *A Pattern Language*.

I was very impressed with his background and story. I told Russ a little about the college I was envisioning and planning to build. Russ said to me, "Form follows function." He explained that simple phrase was one of the first and most important principles of architecture. He asked me to describe in detail what the school hoped to accomplish. As I explained my vision in detail, Russ created a functional diagram of the school:

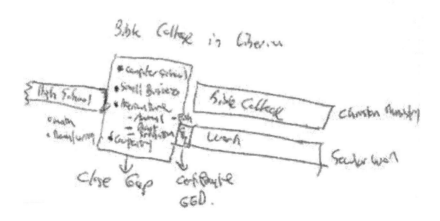

Bible College Functional Diagram

It is hard to imagine LICC without the guidance and perspective Russ has provided over the years in so many areas, but his first contribution was the rough design of the college.

This simple drawing was the first visualization of a building plan for LICC. It should come as no surprise that God has used Russ' passion and experience to design several buildings on the LICC campus as well as the current Campus Master Plan. This project plan was foundational to launching the school, its policies and procedures, the ULICAF and LICC websites, and more.

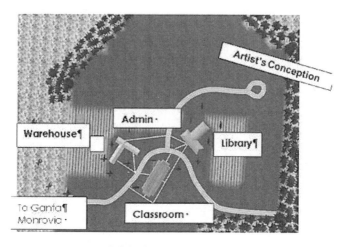

Original Master Plan

Russ jokingly refers to himself as ULICAF/LICC's concierge, saying,

> *At ULICAF/LICC, there are people 'in front' such as the Executive Director. That is how God gifted those people. I'm a 'behind-the-scenes' person who is privileged and honored to provide the support that they need. When people ask me what I do for ULICAF/LICC, I always joke that I'm 'the concierge'—I do whatever they need me to do.*

Of course, all this did not happen in one evening. Russ and I met over coffee for a strategic planning meetings many Wednesday nights. In these meetings, we began tossing ideas around for the design of the college and its buildings, and eventually, many other issues of importance to the college and, to this day, many years later, we have continued our weekly meetings for fellowship and planning.

We also discussed practical methods of implementing the plan, specifically, how we could break down the development into stages and what we would do in each stage over a number of years. Russ helped us prepare our original master plan for LICC. As of this writing we are working on our next five-year formal plan (our third one).

From the beginning, we established what we thought were realistic timelines for these building projects. Our original plan was to have a functioning school in 5 to 10 years. As we break each plan into short term goals (the initial classroom building, then a library, and then a resource center, a clinic, etc.) the Board members and our donors gain a sense of where we are and where we are going. By comparing our plan to what we actually did, we can determine our progress and adjust accordingly. Since we have accomplished most our early goals and see God's hand in providing, we have more confidence to face future building and operational challenges and to budget our resources well.

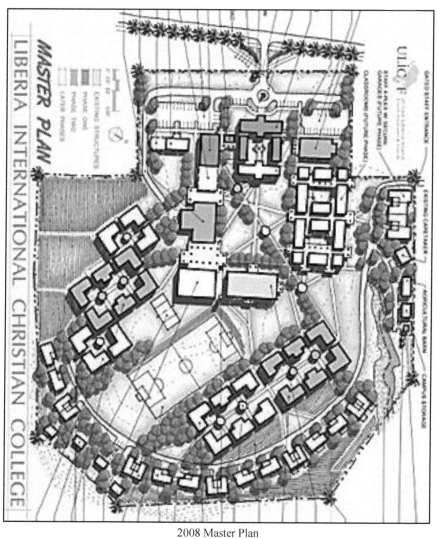

2008 Master Plan

In the past five years (2009-2014), LICC has achieved considerable success. Our goal was to create a college where Liberians could go to study the Bible and learn professional skills. With the help of God and ULICAF's partners we have succeeded:

- When LICC opened its doors in March 2009, 74 students started classes. At the start of the Fall 2013 semester, student enrollment had grown to 220, a 297% increase.

- Similarly, the size of the faculty and staff increased by 475% from 8 faculty and staff in 2009 to 38—20 faculty and 18 staff—in the autumn of 2013.

- On January 29, 2012, LICC held its first graduation and awarded Associate Degrees to 55 students.

Also in the past five years, LICC has:

- Added a second floor to the classroom building.

- Started an on-campus medical clinic to serve students, faculty, and staff.

- Constructed the Faculty Guest House.

- Constructed and moved into the Community Research Center with its first floor library and second floor online learning center.

- Added an agricultural education program, including the purchase of four additional acres for a demonstration farm, and started construction on an Agricultural Education center.

Faculty Guest House

Moving into the Community Resource Center

Planting Beans on the Demonstration Farm

Some of our plans have obviously taken longer than expected while others were completed more quickly. For example, so many good things progressed at LICC during 2013 that the 2012 LICC Master Plan for the campus became obsolete.

The launching of the Agricultural Science program has changed the face of the campus. The southeast side of campus has been transformed with our new *demonstration farm* that includes row crop fields, a greenhouse, a chicken house, and a large rabbit hutch. The 3 lowland acres along the southeast border were purchased to build fish ponds. About an acre was also purchased on the southwest corner to build a well-watered garden.

Chicken House, Rabbit Hutches, and Greenhouse

Garden and Pond with Chicken House to Left,
Water Tower and Campus Buildings in Background

Newly planted field

Beautiful Fountain

Travis Sheets, the Agriculture Program Director, also is skilled at landscape architecture. He designed and constructed a beautiful fountain and flower garden in the center of campus.

Browning Day Mullins Dierdorf Architects of Indianapolis generously offered their design services for a beautiful chapel that we hope to construct in phases over the years to come.

All this amazing growth LICC has experienced has been based on our first and second strategic plans (designed for 2010 to 2014). In order to accomplish the ever-increasing student needs, we set goals in 3 areas that all colleges require: Facilities, Staff, and Students. I outlined some of these goals in my first book, *No More War: Rebuilding Liberia through Faith, Determination & Education.* I will now review them briefly because I am very pleased with our progress, although, of course, we always have ongoing projects to complete.

## PHYSICAL FACILITIES

We worked diligently with our Board to create a long-term Master Plan that included additional areas that were not part of our original Master Plan.

**Our goals (and completion schedule) for the 2010 Strategic Plan:**

- complete construction of the 2nd floor of original building to add 7 more classrooms and offices, and furnish those rooms [*completed*]

- supply textbooks to a growing student body and faculty [*ongoing*]

- increase the collections of the library, purchase needed office supplies, and acquire adequate computers [*completed and ongoing for the new library*]

- install outdoor lighting and landscaping of trees and plants [*ongoing*]

- create visible signage on the road [*completed*]

- provide a purified water system throughout the campus. [started but *not completed*]

**Our goals for 2015 and beyond:**

- Furnish and equip the library and technology center which will also provide internet service for the campus and provide library and technology services to the Ganta community [*Both the library and technology center were dedicated on July 6, 2014.*]

- Construct a health center that will serve as a community health clinic to provide service to both the local Ganta community and the school [*ongoing more urgently since the Ebola Virus Crisis*]

## FACULTY AND STAFF

**Our goals for the 2010 Strategic Plan were:**

- to increase the number of professors in theology, business, and education [*completed*]

- to add an administrator to work with the LICC Management Team [*Gina Sheets, an American missionary from Frankfort, Indiana, was appointed as the Vice President of Administration on March 4, 2014.*]

- to confirm an Academic Dean and a Dean of Students [*We now have a Dean of Student Affairs, Zawolo Zuagele. We are still searching for a Vice President of Academic Affairs.*]

- to provide professional seminars for the development of staff on a regular basis [*not completed*]

- to provide a more detailed job description and qualifications for each teaching position [*not complete*]

Our plan was that by 2010 our faculty would include enough full-time and part-time instructors (either on-site or abroad) to teach the required courses for the curriculum for degrees in Business, Christian Education and Pastoral Studies.

By 2015 we will have established a professional development program to encourage our lecturers to get a master's or doctorate degree either online or on campus at a nearby university. Our goal is that all the instructors for these programs listed above and the courses required for those degrees would be in place for our first full graduating class. We continue to identify qualified instructors for all our programs.

## STUDENTS

**Our goals for the 2010 Strategic Plan were:**

- Increasing scholarship and grant funding for students [*ongoing, but not complete, but a number of students are now receiving scholarships and partial support from the government*]

- transportation (cars and vans) that would be available to students and staff for a small fee [*partially completed with the purchase of a school bus*]

- develop a much-needed *internship/ partnership* program in churches, parachurch organizations, businesses, and government for our graduates with Associate's or Bachelor's degrees [*ongoing*]

- fully implement the Bachelor's degrees in Pastoral Studies, Christian Education, and Business; starting other majors [*ongoing*]

**Beyond 2015, the student goals include:**

- Have a functional agricultural farm to teach better farming practices and to produce fruits and vegetables for the school and for sale to the community. [*parts are complete and all is ongoing since the agricultural department is well under way*]

## The Big Strategic Plan

**Ongoing Needs:**

- We need excellent security for our computers/data and our buildings to provide for the safety of the students and faculty.

- We need drinking water that is safe.

- We will have ongoing communication needs to explain the growth of the school to our constituents, the community, and prospective students.

- We will begin the process of setting up scholarships for students and endowment plans that will fund the salaries of our instructors.

- We will strengthen our relationships with our donor base and pursue funding through a wider network of philanthropy organizations and foundations that offer grants for universities like ours.

- We will continue developing our relationships within the local community that we are dedicated to helping.

**Long Term Vision:**

ULICAF and the LICC anticipate a bright future. Our dreams include:

- Strategic partnerships with other colleges and universities for access to professors and courses

- Installation of high-speed internet connection throughout the campus

- Construction of a student center, a chapel, and additional faculty housing

- Launch of a Nursing School and construction of a clinic on the front side of the campus

- Accreditation to offer Bachelor of Arts degrees

- Launch a Vocational Training Program and construct a vocational school

- For a more detailed description of the LICC Campus Master Plan, view it in the "downloads" section of the ULICAF web site (www.ulicaf.org)

As we continue to commit our plans to Him and seek His path (and *timing*), we believe that we will accomplish our goals and impact and educate an ever increasing number of Liberians.

# The "Elevator Speech"

In the United States, I first learned about an "elevator speech." The elevator speech does not, of course, have to be used on an elevator, but it should not be longer than an elevator ride; one must be able to state one's vision or passion in a few minutes. It must be a clear, concise, and focused statement. My elevator speech is a quick overview of what our organization is all about—both what we plan to accomplish and how we plan to do it. Not all parts are important to all listeners, so it can be adapted for different people.

When I meet someone casually who might be interested in ULICAF, I'm respectful of their time. A brief way that I share the vision for those interested is:

My Current Elevator Speech:

> We are an organization of both Liberian refugees and their American friends who are helping to rebuild Liberia by building a college. Liberia has recently gone through a 15-year devastating civil war (now ended) that killed thousands of our people. And also, many professionals and educators left the country, creating educational needs.
>
> For leadership, we are currently working on my transition to Liberia. We are also working on finding a new Executive Director for the U.S. office. For our projects, our current priorities are to equip the library and the technology center, finish our agricultural center, build a community health center, and finally, build a student center.
>
> We have made an application for LICC to go from an associate's degree to a bachelor's degree program,

increase from 200 students to 350 students, and to hire 3 to 5 professors with Master's degrees.

Truth@work, under the leadership of Perry Hines and Ray Hilbert, have helped me with these elevator speeches and one-page business plans. Ray Hilbert funded my two-year study time with other non-profit organizations to help me develop into a more competent and skillful leader. I met with leaders of operating non-profits to learn strategic lessons on what works and what not to do.

## Developing a One-Page Business Plan

As part of that program, I developed a one-page business plan. This is a longer, written version of the elevator speech. A basic one-page business plan includes:

- *Vision - what we want to accomplish*: We want to establish a college with 3 buildings where over 100 students could be trained in biblical studies, business, agriculture, teaching, or nursing.

- *Mission - what we exist to do*: Educate Liberians who might not otherwise have access to a college education.

- *Objectives - measurable future goals*: Build a classroom building with 6 classrooms; get accreditation as a two-year institution; recruit 50 students; hire 4 teachers.

- *Strategies - or how we would produce the results and ensure long-term success*: Raise money from both the Liberian refugee community and our American friends; purchase land in Ganta with a down payment; ask the community and students to partner with us to construct the building; and finally, avoid long-term debt by breaking our plan into small manageable pieces.

- *Action Plans - what steps we need to take to meet deadlines:* Raise $10,000 at our annual banquet in November; hire 2 new professors before the start of the next term; start a medical clinic by December.

Formal 50-page business plans are important for bank loans, but initially our supporters and churches needed to get an idea of what our vision really was. This 1-page business plan also was an excellent planning tool that kept us on track. I highly recommend creating a focused one-page business plan to anyone starting a new venture.

# Chapter 7:  Starting at the Beginning

## The First Step: Purchase Land

We had a vision and the very beginnings of a plan we believed in. From the very beginning I vowed not to ask anyone for money unless we ourselves, as Liberian refugees, invested the "seed money" to get started.

Of course, it would have been nice to have had one big donor who gave us enough cash to buy land and begin construction at once. But we had many lessons to learn about faith, patience, and how God raises up many people with their varied talents to build a college. Plants are started from seed; they do not spring out of the earth fully mature in one day and ready for harvesting.   Just as plants need time, water, nutrients, and sun, our college needed time, peoples' prayers, peoples' talents, and relationships to become a working entity.

We realized that to accomplish this "big vision" of educating students to qualify for jobs that would positively impact Liberia, we needed a campus full of buildings and instructors and technology. We also needed a source (or many sources) of funding for the construction of these buildings and payment of teacher salaries. The future students needed money to attend the college.

What was the first step we needed to take to make LICC a reality? The obvious step was to buy land! Just because Liberia was a third world country did not necessarily mean land was cheap, but we had the faith to believe God would give us the money to purchase some land and He would lead us to the right land to purchase.

## Monrovia: Yes or No?

But where should the school be located? Monrovia, the capital? We completely ruled out Monrovia; we would have been just one of many colleges already there. There was only one university located in central

Liberia (outside of Monrovia) that offered quality education, but it was very expensive like most Liberian colleges. It was just a fact that most Liberians never go to college—not because of lack of desire but because of the large obstacles to overcome – travel distances and cost.

For example, the rural area where I grew up had very few people who could afford to go beyond high school. Most rural Liberians worked very hard, went to high school, and then returned to the village to work on the family subsistence farm. They never made use of more than a primary education in reading, math, and science.

In 2010, when Yah and I made our first return visit to Liberia, a good friend Nathaniel and his son Ashmun came to see me at LICC—with tears in his eyes. Nathaniel's wife had died during the civil war from an illness that could have been easily prevented if there had been medical service available. Nathaniel was left with eleven children. His education had not extended beyond elementary school and he did not sit for the Grade 6 National exam, so technically, he didn't complete that. Of his children, Ashmun was the only son who had managed to finish high school. Even so, Ashmun could not obtain his transcript because he could not afford the *final* payment to the school.

Ashmun and his father had come to us to appeal for help. They did not want any handout from me and Yah, but they did want our help with this one thing: getting Ashmun into college.

Ashmun and Nathaniel

On my return to the United States, I wrote about Ashmun in our newsletter and someone volunteered to contribute to Ashmun's tuition. Additionally, Ashmun received one of our *One Hour for Christ Scholarships* and entered the United Methodist University in Monrovia to pursue a nursing degree.

Ashmun is now doing his internship at the Methodist Hospital in Ganta and has three more semesters to complete his study! This is one of our many success stories.

## Choosing the City of Ganta

The question, then, that was nagging at my soul and others I knew was: "Should not Liberia have more colleges outside of Monrovia?" If not Monrovia, where in Liberia should we start? We recognized that the majority of Liberians did not live in the capital city. How was a person going to have an opportunity if he or she lived outside of Monrovia?

We considered many places, but finally decided on the city of Ganta. We knew that there was a large pool of prospective students from this large rural city of about sixty-thousand.

Since the college would be located close to their homes, they would not have large travel expenses. Those who moved to Ganta would be able to fine affordable housing. We also had decided that building dormitories and a cafeteria would distract us from our main focus of teaching. Since our students would need a place to sleep and food to eat, Ganta provided enough resources and housing for these potential students to live nearby and attend the school. There would even be places they or their spouses could work and schools their children could attend.

Even more important, Ganta was a crossroads for Liberia. When someone leaves Monrovia to travel to southern Liberia, they usually have to go through Ganta. Similarly, when someone is going to Monrovia, they will usually go through Ganta, often stopping to get food or to rest.

If the government would have money to spend on infrastructure, Ganta would likely be one of the first places to receive it. From Ghana there are electric poles going to the south. Over the years, as we have continued to build LICC, we have seen some of our projections come to pass. For example, in 2013, the first regional government-funded electricity lighted the streets of the city of Ganta. Currently, they are working to bring electricity into homes. LICC is already included in the plan to receive electricity! As of this printing, LICC now has electricity and is no longer dependent on its generators.

Another advantage in choosing Ganta was the substantial number of professional people who could be hired part-time or as adjunct instructors. For example, there were banks and hospitals in Ganta. As the need and opportunity arose, we hoped that some of these professionals would help us as business and finance instructors. We also hoped that some of the doctors and nurses would help out at the college clinic. In addition to this, we expected to find instructors from some of the Non-Government Organizations (NGOs) working in and around Ganta. As we were just starting up, we knew realistically we would not be able to employ many *full-time* people, so, we would need to recruit faculty from the local community. Ganta seemed like a place that would have a pool of potential part-time faculty from many different sources and professions.

## "Casting a Fleece"

Once we decided on the area of Ganta, we asked church leaders in Liberia to "put out a fleece" to see if they could help us find a parcel of land for the school. The concept of fleece is mentioned in the Bible (Judges 6:36-40). Following Gideon's victories (tearing down of Baal's altar and his later attack against the Midianites), he got a call to lead the delivery of the children of Israel from ferocious enemy forces. He then devised two tests whereby he would know beyond all doubt that the Lord would save Israel by his hand. So, he placed a wool fleece on the threshing floor overnight. If it was wet with dew in the morning and all the ground around it dry, that would indicate God's confirmation to save Israel by his hand.

In our case, our confidence in God's promises was unwavering, but we fervently wanted God's affirmation that our plan to build a college in Ganta was of Him and not of our own desires. God did answer us God in His mercy answered our request by showing our leaders a suitable piece of land in the city of Ganta. The leadership of ULICAF felt this was God's confirmation, solidifying our commitment to the mission He had set before us.

The church leaders first contacted the local churches to see if anyone had a piece of land. We also were looking for someone to make an initial down payment. We had raised some money, but not enough to buy a large enough piece of land.

Amazingly, and in God's will and timing, we found that land! How did people react when we had found our land? As you would expect, they were ecstatic. Many friends were saying that since we had found the land, we should go ahead and buy it. The Board had approved the decision, so of course, we did buy it. We purchased this property outright on the outskirts of Ganta for $12,000. Most of the money came from an earlier gift from Christ Memorial Church in Holland, Michigan. This church had been my home church and supported my family and me through many hard times in the beginning. They had remained strongly attached to the vision for LICC. They had set aside a sum of money for us from their Thanksgiving offerings, and we used some of that money to buy the land.

Map of the Area

## Future Expansion

We wish we had purchased more land because at the time the property was surrounded mostly by forest. In a few short years, the city has grown around us. People have started to build houses.

There is a life lesson in this as well. Sometimes we dream too small, but we are thankful to have at least purchased 20 acres! We bought what we could afford. You might think the story would end here with the 20 acres of land, but it did not.

In the spring of 2013, while walking around the campus, I noticed that several adjacent landowners had built homes or laid foundations as close as 30 feet from the school's property line. Our concern was that their building on this land would encroach on the school property. Although the initial development of the land was mainly residential, Liberia is different than America. In Liberia, you can put anything on your property without going through approval by a local or county planning commission. For example, one of the plots could have become a liquor store or used for some other type of business not in harmony with our school's vision. Legally, we would not be able to challenge them.

I learned that Hope College in Holland, Michigan, began buying land and houses surrounding their college so they could be ready for future expansion. Thus, I began to consider how we might be proactive in preparing for the future.

I invited the property owners to a meeting and expressed my concern and offered them the opportunity to relocate so that the college could expand. I called the ULICAF Board members and informed them of the opportunity and I obtained their approval. The school successfully negotiated with all the property owners and we purchased a total of 4.5 acres with a $25,000 donation from a generous ULICAF friend. The largest parcel, located near the back of the campus, is swamp land that can accommodate 25 to 30 fish ponds. Raising fish will generate income for school. Rice is the main staple of Liberian food. However, next on the list of staples is meat. Liberians like fish and meat, particularly the meat of wild animals. As for fish, most Liberians would eat fish every day if they had access to it and could afford it. So, if we start raising catfish, there would be an instant market for this. We also hope to raise chickens and other animals. These new parcels will be part of the agriculture demonstration farm, and retail fish sales will generate additional revenue for the LICC. A smaller parcel near the front of the campus will be used for a well-watered garden.

At the end of a recent trip to Liberia, one of our students introduced me to another landowner who had a building located on the south side of our demonstration farm. The student had explained that LICC is expanding and would buy his land if he would be willing to be relocate. The landowner agreed and came to see me. So, we continue to negotiate to acquire more land for future expansion. As I returned to the States, pondering over the land deals, I remembered the words of the Psalmist, "The steps of a good man are ordered by the Lord, and he delights in His way" (Psa. 37:23). We knew in our hearts that more doors would open to accommodate future students.

# Chapter 8: Our Volunteers and Financial Donors

LICC would not exist today if many people had not given of their time and money.

## Inspiring People to Give of Their Time

ULICAF stands for <u>United Liberian Inland Church</u> <u>Associates and Friends</u>. What does it mean to be an "associate" or a "friend"? ULICAF has no formal membership, and there are no annual fees to maintain one's membership. But an associate or friend is someone who believes in our mission of helping Liberia and wants to stay informed and connected with us through our various forms of correspondence such as email and monthly newsletters. Many of these friends/associates regularly pray for us. Some of these friends even go on mission trips to Liberia. Others help us in various other ways.

Our friends financially support our vision, some by contributing regularly and some by donating to special projects, and some do both. Initially, most of these associates were from the Liberian refugee community and knew about the hard conditions and struggles and needs we all had. (Some children, though, were too young when they left to remember these hardships—or they were born in America.) So, we all gave generously of our time and money. We looked at these refugees as our "associates." Our "friends" are all the other wonderful Christians who, though they did not experience Liberian civil war, believed they were called by God to come alongside us to help and encourage us.

It took countless hours, and even months, to share our struggles and history with these new American friends so they could really understand our recent past and the pain we experienced and connect with our passion to rebuild our country. This is the main reason we have written two books to give a good summary of our history and some of the amazing stories of survival and answers to prayer.

## Direct Contact

As a leader, I learned from my African culture that "relationships" are the foundation for successfully building any organization. And our first volunteers came from those we met in churches and God impressed a desire upon their hearts to want to know me and my story. Many of these volunteers then shared with their friends and soon we had more people that believed in our vision.

As the Executive Director, I shared my passion with everyone I met. I told them about my vision to not only educate a nation of future Liberian leaders, but also help build integrity and character into them. I needed to win the trust of my new friends, so I shared exactly how I planned to use their monetary gifts. If I said that I was raising funds to buy a piece of land, I did exactly that—even if there were other legitimate ministry needs. I would be tested many times, but I faithfully waited until we could buy our first plot of land. I tirelessly explained how we are not just educating, although that is a worthwhile endeavor in itself, but we also care about building character. We are in the business of sharing our faith in a way that will build better Liberian leaders for the future.

Where did we find some of these first faithful volunteers? About 90% of all the women involved with ULICAF in Indianapolis were friends of my wife, Yah—women she met through various Bible studies she attended. She met many others at church or in the community. These women were instrumental in planning our banquets which were very important to our fundraising efforts. Without my loving, faithful, hard-working wife I would not have been able to be as successful in getting this vison off the ground.

Ladies from Indiana Enjoy a Visit to LICC

## Stories of Changed Lives

In February 2014, Byron Miller from Illinois accepted our request to teach Managerial Accounting for four weeks at LICC. During his stay, he shared how he got connected to ULICAF.

> *I had never been to Liberia and learned about ULICAF from Wesley and Mercy Lankah who are members of my church in Glen Ellyn, IL. Last fall, they invited Dr. Buor to come up and speak to us during a potluck lunch after church. I was intrigued by his message of hope for Liberia and especially for Ganta. I spoke with him afterwards and on the way home said to my wife, 'When Dr. Buor puts his hand on you, you cannot escape.'*

> *I taught Managerial Accounting and due to textbooks not arriving in time, I was only equipped with 12 copies of Managerial Accounting for Dummies that were purchased at the last minute to bring with me. I found my students to be eager, on-time, and quite*

*willing to speak up and ask questions in the class. I learned to be more flexible and more carefully attuned to the students' situation.*

*I am reminded of a song that we sang when I was a child: "Brighten the Corner Where You Are." Remember that whatever the conditions today, we're working for a brighter tomorrow. Does not the Bible teach us to work for the edification of all around us?*

In sharing the vision of LICC, I wanted to do more than tell my story or the survival and success stories of other Liberians. We have been very encouraged by hearing how involvement with ULICAF has changed peoples' lives. When other Christians hear of excitement over the growth of ULICAF and LICC, many others want to get involved.

We are creating messengers for LICC—people who have gotten involved, found it a fulfilling experience, and as a result, brought to us new "friends" of the ministry.

## Short Term Trips

How do we do this? First of all, we encourage people to visit LICC, and see firsthand what has been done already in Liberia at LICC. Once there, many catch the vision of using their gifts and talents and educational background to help us.

Beth Helps with Knitting Class

Our IT volunteer, Bob Henninger, has gone to Liberia 3 times. Bob, who is recently retired, did not renew his apartment lease so that he could go for an even longer period! As you can imagine, he keeps coming back because he finds meaning and purpose in training Liberians on computers.

In 2012, I spoke at a Presbyterian church near Indianapolis and I asked Bob to come along and share his experiences. Because he was an educated American who grew up in the Midwest, like most of our audience that night, he was able to connect with them even more than I. It was easier for them to see themselves doing what Bob was doing than it was to imitate me or another Liberian. Those in the congregation that night came to understand that if a humble man like Bob could use his availability and talents to help Liberians, maybe they could donate some of their time.

Another example of this was a group that came over to visit our agriculture project and planted about beans and some trees on the campus. Though this was very difficult labor working in the hot Liberian sun, our campus now has wonderful shade which adds life and beauty to our campus. These loving Christians have the satisfaction of helping in the creation of the beautiful LICC campus in a very tangible way.

## Leveraging the Passions of Volunteers

Sometimes it is just a matter of finding the right person for the job. When people become involved with ULICAF, we encourage them to participate in ways that align with their passions and abilities and God's will for their lives. Then, we work to provide them with experiences that match their passions. Many have told us how rewarding it has been spiritually as they use their gifts to help those less fortunate than themselves in a third world country.

There is no better example of this than Russ Schwartz. He had a passion for architecture, even though he had a career working with computers. Russ designed most of our first building and we challenged him to fulfill a dream of his.

When we got Russ as a volunteer we had no idea that he would recruit a very close friend of his to become our first accountant. It was his wife, Ruth! Little did I know that indeed that my first landlords when I moved to Carmel in Central Indiana would be my most faithful supporters and advisors. Russ Schwartz built a structure that has lasted us through the years and Ruth to this day keeps our books and files our annual reports.

## Our Key Donors

Ongoing financial gifts were, and are, crucial to the funding of the construction of LICC's campus buildings. Here again, we started with the small "seed money" donations of Liberians. I want to emphasize that the Liberian refugee community gave generously to ULICAF and LICC. Without their sacrificial giving, we never would have even launched the ministry.

Even though the building costs are lower in Liberia than America, it still takes a lot of money to build a college. Most of our key donors gave to ULICAF and LICC after hearing our story from our conferences, from me when I spoke to a church or group, or directly from personal contact. We will be eternally thankful for those churches and American and European friends who gave generously to provide the funds to propel us forward.

ULICAF has received many large gifts over the years. I would like to list a few of them and why they were important to us.

### *Christ Memorial Church in Holland, Michigan*

When I first started raising money, I made an appointment with Dr. Gordon Van Wylen, the President of Hope College. I wanted to talk to him about developing a funding strategy. He had taken me under his wing when I was a theology student at Western Theological Seminary, and he has helped me again and again.

Since I was a member of Christ Memorial Church in Holland, Michigan, our first grant proposal was written to that church. They generously donated an initial sum of $28,000! This greatly encouraged us to believe that our seemingly impossible big dreams were actually possible. Furthermore, since we neither had a 501(c)3 status, nor the immediate need to spend the money, the church created an account to hold the money for us until the time when we could purchase land in Liberia.

## *Northwest Covenant Church in Mount Prospect, Illinois*

When it was time to dedicate myself to full-time ministry for ULICAF, I sent out letters to many contacts to raise support. I received a letter back from Northwest Covenant Church in Mount Prospect, Illinois. They included a check for a substantial amount to go toward my support. In the letter the mission board chair explained that the funds were from their *own* Liberia ministry account. This was another confirmation of what God was planning for Liberia and that, if we trusted God and obeyed Him alone, He would provide future partners to support us. Since then, Covenant church pastors, Dr. Helb Jacobsen and Rev. Paul Thompson (the current senior pastor) have both visited us in Liberia to see the fruit that has resulted from their gifts as well as the gifts of others.

A Covenant member called me and said, "What have you done to our pastor? He is changed. What happened in Liberia?" Since that visit, they have committed to ongoing support for LICC which has inspired others in their church to catch the vison of rebuilding this civil-war-torn nation.

## *Grace Church, Noblesville, Indiana*

In 2006, we decided to host a Liberian Christian conference in Indianapolis. Fortunately, through my wife Yah, I made the acquaintance of a women's Bible study leader. This leader encouraged the women in several other Bible studies she led to support our conference by hosting a banquet. At that banquet we raised over $27,000 for LICC. Since that time she has continued to give to us generously as well as helping us raise financial support.

Besides this money, Grace Church and its members contributed $18,000 toward installing plumbing, laying floor tiles, and painting the second floor of our Classroom Building. In fact, Grace Church in Noblesville, has been extravagantly generous over the years to help us meet ongoing financial challenges for the building of new campus buildings and furnishing classrooms.

### *Donors Inspired by First Book,* No More War

A good book goes a long way! When I first went out and spoke about ULICAF and our dream for LICC, I noticed that other speakers had pamphlets and even personal testimony books documenting their vision and journey. I did have a well-written short pamphlet, but not a complete book of my story and vision. Several friends encouraged me to write a book—which eventually I did.

That first book, *No More War*, told about my history and explained our vision for a new college in Liberia. One of our largest individual donations was the result of that book. A friend who was in the financial consulting business gave a copy of that book to several of his clients. God did an amazing thing. One of his clients was looking for a place to donate some money. His wife was quite inspired by my story and then shared the book with her husband. Together they donated $50,000. This covered a substantial portion of the expense of the second floor of our first building.

Prior to this gift, a U.S.-based foundation had accepted our grant request, but would only give us a matching grant. Every dollar that we raised for the classroom building would be matched up to $50,000—which would be a total contribution of $100,000. This generous and timely gift made it possible for us to receive that grant, and then to complete the second floor of the classroom building.

## _Liberian Refugee Donations_

One of our largest individual donations came from a Liberian refugee who came to America and committed himself to pursuing an education. Today, as a dentist in the United States, he is far removed from the abject poor refuge who arrived so many years ago. Being thankful to God for the opportunity to study in the U.S. and grateful for all his blessings today, he never forgot his home country and their needs. He generously donated $25,000 to ULICAF for LICC. In addition, he contributed $20,000 toward a church currently under construction in his home area in Liberia. I had the privilege of breaking ground for it in March, 2013. This Liberian has now contributed more than $45,000.

## Accepting Donations in a 501(c)(3) Organization

In order for an individual donor to receive a tax-deductible receipt for his contribution it must be given to 501(c)(3) not-for-profit organization. When we started out, we did not have that IRS status and initially relied on Phil and Amber Snyder of Holland, Michigan. Phil was the first partner of our ministry (ULICAF). He used his 501(c)(3) tax exempt ministry, Glow Ministries International (GLOW), to accept our gifts until we obtained our own not-for-profit status.

Later, when we moved to Indiana, a minister at Grace Church helped us to get set up to receive funds through Grace. Through the encouragement of Jon Lieberman at Grace Church, we started pursuing this long process, and eventually we became a bona fide tax-exempt ministry.

# Chapter 9: Developing Organizational Partnerships

Resources are limited and our dreams are big, so whenever and wherever we can, we look for organizational partners. One of our foundational strategies is to be open to those types of opportunities.

The basic search for organizational partners happens in one of two ways. Sometimes we are contacted by people or organizations that believe we should work together. In other cases, we go looking for partners for a specific strategic need. ULICAF leaders and I give presentations on our mission on a regular basis. That is how organizations learn about ULICAF and make their first contact with us. Other times, friends of ULICAF connect us with people or organizations they think would be interested in our mission. Regardless of how we are connected, we look forward to these contacts because they have yielded a number of good partnerships.

I receive many, many calls. If the call is about something we are interested in incorporating into ULICAF or LICC, I follow up to discern the person's (or organization's) heart and passion. Many times they are not a good fit for ULICAF; some are worthy of further discussion.

## Our Needs in Organizational Partners

ULICAF exists to transform Liberia and the world for Christ. We see partnership as a relationship between people and ministries who share like visions and aspirations, are willing to strive to achieve them together, and do so in a spirit of co-operation and brotherly love. The first expectation, above all else is "Christ alone and equals." For us, this means that we are all equal in Christ, there is no superiority of one Christian over another.

We believe this so strongly, that we consider the individuals and their ministries to be our partners. We partner with Christ followers and Christian organizations nationally (Liberia) and around the world. When our partner succeeds in bringing healing to broken Liberia and the world, *ULICAF WINS*.

- We partner with missionaries who are full-time workers for God and called to transform the "broken" world, and depend on God for their provision.

- We partner with organizations with a clear ministry purpose— organizations that are held accountable by a board of directors who oversees the organization's mission and direction.

- We partner with individuals or professionals who are asking God to effectively use their gifts where they are most needed.

As we started building LICC, it did not take long for us to realize that we would need far more borrowed talents, time, and treasures than we had, so we asked our current friends and donors to help raise more partners. As the saying goes, *"Friends raise friends."*

## Waiting on God's Timing and Leading

We do everything in our power to ensure that the relationship will be a good match. Our relationship with Training Leaders International (TLI) is an example of a good partnership we have formed. In late 2009, I was connected with Dr. Howard Foreman in California through a mutual friend. Howard was fresh out of university, having earned his PhD in Church History at the University of Aberdeen in Scotland. When I first contacted him, he asked that he be allowed to pray about involvement with us. I did not hear back for quite some time. Then one day an email appeared in my mailbox from Howard:

> *I do not know if you remember me, but you contacted me, maybe 2 years ago concerning doing some teaching at your university. Today, I am a part of Training Leaders International (TLI), an organization birthed out of John Piper's Church. We are the*

*overseas arm and we pursue the vision of training pastors. We send teams overseas to train pastors and leaders, both on a short and long term basis. We are looking into opportunities for the coming year and wonder if there might be an occasion to talk about possibilities in Liberia. We bring seminary professors, pastors and even seminary students (who need experience and a heart for missions) and we work with existing organizations in their ongoing efforts (and sometimes start new works, too) to build the body of Christ worldwide.*

Dr. Howard Freeman

In 2012, Dr. Freeman led a team of four (including himself) and taught various theological courses at LICC. In 2014, we received another team of three from TLI. TLI is preparing another team under the leadership of Dr. Tom Brown to come and teach at LICC beginning in February, 2016.

Later, I'll discuss our expectations and formal process for evaluating partners and building relationships. Here I would like to discuss some of our guiding principles for finding partners.

## Shared Vision, Faith and Values

When we share a vision with an organization or individual, that establishes clarity of purpose and exerts a sense of gravity that aligns our actions and keep us moving in the same direction. I am using vision here to mean a picture of the future that is both compelling and credible. Shared vision involves the guidance around what will be accomplished and who will benefit from the endeavor.

An excellent example of the value of shared vision, faith, and mutual respect is Evangelical Theological Seminary of Indonesia (ETSI). ETSI was established in 1978 as a dream of Chris Marantika, an Indonesian seminary student who had gone to the United States to study. Allen Finley, CEO of Partners International, partnered with Chris, as Allen believed Chris was ordained by God. Allen treated Chris with dignity and supported Chris's dream. Allen believed from the start that his investment in Chris would not only benefit Chris, but also benefit Indonesians and the work of the gospel. Today, there are 30 branches (20 Bible Colleges and 10 seminaries) all over Indonesia, with a combined total of over 4,000 students. Chris's dream came to be known as "Vision Indonesia 1:1:1" and Chris continues to lead that organization.

Building a shared vision consists of assembling a team of workers who have the desire to accomplish a shared goal and the skills to pursue that desire. All the team members are under one banner—Christ alone; the players are equals. Partnership is not an invitation to someone to come and help someone else. "Helping" someone often assumes a one-sided view of the other person and the relationship. In the worst cases, helping leads to the giving party feeling superior to those they help and the person or organization being helped feels inferior or beholden. Partnership, on the other hand, is working together. Partnership is a "collaboration" to fulfill God's call. When we are one under "Christ's banner," we are "equals," showing the world by our love for one another that we are Christ's disciples (John 13:35).

As we seek partners, we look for people who believe that we wait on God, but that we do not make God wait on us. We have had to and are continuing to exercise a lot of faith in this. Our partners should be following the path God has for them. If they are, it should turn out good in the end. We like those we partner with to be open to steps of faith. We need to do our part—at least to do what God expects of us.

*He has shown you, O mortal, what is good. And what does the Lord require of you? To act justly and to love mercy and to walk humbly with your God.* Micah 6:8 (NIV)

Our point is that if we do not obey God, there will be challenges in our physical world. God will try to get us back on the right path. Unless believers can put faith into action, God is never going to go in motion for them. Personally, I had every reason to stay in the United States and find a permanent job, but God moved me to take these steps forward. We did not start with all the resources, but God made people available to bring resources and help us advance His kingdom.

As a Christian liberal arts college, we are interested in building relationships with those who align with our faith-based beliefs. The Bible talks about being unequally yoked with the unbeliever. However, I will not say we would not partner with a non-Christian organization because that would be limiting God and God may want us to speak a message into their lives. Perhaps in seeing our commitment to helping others they will gain more respect for God and His people. We would be much more careful and seek God's guidance if we were to partner with a non-faith-based person or group.

## Compatibility in Passion and Path

We have found that the best partners are ones whose passions and work they are doing align with the purposes of ULICAF. Passions are not always reflected by the person's profession—a good example of this is Russ Schwartz who worked in information technology, but helped ULICAF and LICC in a myriad of other ways, including one of his great passions of architecture. Passion is important to us because there will be trials along the way, but obstacles are more frequently overcome when one is passionate about attaining the end goal.

By path we mean God's plan for that organization or its people. There are plenty of examples in Genesis of people who are called by God, and who fail miserably along the way. Abraham was a great man of faith, but he sometimes fell short. Abraham's story shows that sometimes the call is easy, but sustaining a steady pace over a long period of time and through complex circumstances is very difficult.

We believe, though, if being involved with us is a part of what God wants for them, we have to be compatible in regard to their passion and our needs. Eventually, Abraham had a son and eventually God fulfilled his promise to Abraham:

> *He took him outside and said, "Look up at the sky and count the stars—if indeed you can count them." Then he said to him, "So shall your offspring be."* Genesis 15:5 (NIV)

But, it was a long, hard road getting there for Abraham and for God's chosen people. Most of our roads at ULICAF and LICC have been much shorter, but from time to time we have faced trials, and we have had to practice patience, or we have had to remain flexible and creative. It is all very much easier if there is alignment of our partners and ourselves around the objectives we plan to achieve, and if ultimately, God can be expected to bless that effort.

## Motivation

We do not want people who are reluctant. That is often a sign that working with us is not God's plan for their lives or organization. Let me give an example. We want to expand our medical clinic, so we are actively working to find a partner in this area. By chance, we came in contact with a medical doctor who had an interest in Liberia. We talked to him and were impressed. He seemed eager to help, willing to make the sacrifices necessary to move over to Ganta and expand our clinic. We thought he might be the answer to our prayers. We wanted to see how his wife felt. Unlike him, his wife was hesitant. Although she was polite, she really did not seem to be curious about this opportunity. From our experience, we know it takes twice the effort if the spouse is not onboard as when the couple are in agreement with God and each other and are working together. God will provide, but God has not provided through this particular doctor.

I cannot convince you if you do not want to go. The Holy Spirit can bring the passion; God can move in people's hearts. He can give people the conviction that human words alone will not bring. If He does not, that probably means that that partnership was not meant to be or the timing was not right.

We made this mistake very early when LICC came into being in 2009. We recruited a retired lady who had skills we needed, but did not have the team mindset or the vision and passion for the people and the work. She lasted for only a semester, and we got lots of complaints from staff and students. She was the only person at LICC who possessed a car—a four-wheel drive jeep. In those days, the city was lighted only with generators. Our classes ran from 9:00 AM to 8:30 PM. We would shut down our generator immediately after classes to save fuel. To our surprise, the instructor refused to give a ride to any student or fellow instructor because she felt she was not responsible for their poverty. Besides, she appeared to feel she had given the Liberian student more than they deserved just by leaving her comfortable home in the United States and coming to teach. A student told me that one day she was in good spirits and gave her a ride. During the ride, the student received a call on her cell phone and decided to answer it. The lady refused to allow her to talk on her cell phone while she was being given the favor of a ride, and threatened to put her out of the car if she answered the call. Our student never answered the call.

## Values and Priorities

Another factor to consider in passion and path is dealing with operational values and ministry priorities. These go beyond belief in Christ and include financial practices, decision making, and respect and dignity for national leaders.

I interviewed an American friend who took a leave of absence from his work and served in Haiti for one whole year. I asked my friend to enlighten me on what he felt it would take to build an effective partnership with our American friends. He said, from the beginning, lay down clear expectations. He went on to name the expectations:

- First, it must be clear that the two partners "are under Christ's banner and are equals," despite their cultural or national backgrounds, education, or material advantages. Establish Jesus's model of authority which requires a balance of power. We are to serve each other. Jesus was God, but came down to serve humanity, and as a result, the Father exalted him. The clear sense of God's call derived from strong conviction and discernment of alignment with the mission is indispensable. The point is that each partner's disposition and temperament ought always to be that of Christ. This truth is also taught at the Last Supper. Jesus recognized all authority has been given to him by his Father, yet he got up and washed the feet of his disciples (John 13:5). Jesus had (and has) a different perspective for the world, and calls us to submit to one another for His name's sake. When we call a partner, it is a call to build God's kingdom together!

- Second, establish "bridge people." These are people who can see both sides of the relationship, both the foreign and American sides. Bridge people should be culturally informed and also genuine. This is because it is important to provide access to genuine truth-tellers who will guide the relationship between the partners and help them see each other's point of view.

- Third, ensure respect for local or national authorities. Then he added, very often American's perception of democracy can make them forget to "live under the Romans" (Phil. 2:5-11). It can lead to disrespect for authorities and a confrontational attitude, even when confrontation is not the best solution. The "battle" we are called to is not an earthly battle but a spiritual one. Just like the kingdom of heaven is not an earthly kingdom, but a spiritual one. There are times to confront authorities, but usually we (and our mission for Christ) are better served if we show respect for authority, live under it, and focus on advancing His kingdom.

- Finally, relationship is essential for productivity. Because of this, it is important to consider how people relate to each other, work together, trust each other, and communicate with each other. You can have compelling values, the latest technology, and a proven strategic plan, but without relationship (without love), you would fail miserably. Look for the right level of individual involvement and also a commitment to relationship.

Like any relationship (marriage comes to mind immediately), it often takes work. For example, with one of our partner's board of directors, we each selected a dedicated and trusted person from our own organization to work together. Their job was to manage the relationship between us and our new partner. For a strong relationship, you must build trust. As part of that, we seek to understand our partner's intentions and their competencies. This helps us trust each other's perspective, and to communicate freely and openly, even if the message is negative.

Once we come to trust each other, it allows us to devote our time to God's work rather than spending inordinate amounts of time in meetings to agree on what we are going to do, and who will do it and when, or worse, sitting around and spreading gossip and fostering prejudices against one another. These are principles that have passed the test of time; they were important back in Nehemiah's day when he rebuilt Jerusalem. The partnership will never go beyond how the partners are getting along.

Building and managing a relationship of trust takes effort. Sometimes it may not seem worth the cost in time and energy. However, the combined effort of the group (partnership) is far greater than what either one could do alone. As people work together in unity, the results are exponentially far greater.

People remain motivated when they feel they belong and are needed. I would state it simply like this: we need each other; there is a unique job for every one of us; and we belong here together. People neither perform their best nor remain committed very long if you make them feel weak, dependent, or alienated. But, when we give our power away and foster their personal power and ownership, they grow stronger and more competent—this is what it means to empower people. When empowered people also have self-determination, amazing things can and do happen.

## Capabilities and Availability

It is good to have passion, and it is good to feel God's calling, but it is also important to have the ability to fulfill the dream. If an organization does not have the prerequisite resources, it is difficult to maintain the partnership. Often we can provide some type of support to our partners or help with transportation or a place to live, but we rarely can provide all the support they will need. We have been fortunate to find many organizations, and thus many volunteers, that have been willing to make personal sacrifices to help us build LICC. Similarly, we are looking for help with our medical clinic. No matter the passion or desire, someone without a medical background (a doctor or nurse) is unlikely to be a good fit. That is an extreme example, but I think you get the picture. If they have no medical background, then they would need to find someone who does, and partner with them to bring a proposal to us.

Gina Sheets, Sue Ellspermann, Indiana Governor Mike Pence

Lieutenant Governor Sue Ellspermann, who under state statute serves as the Secretary of Agriculture, appointed Gina Sheets as ISDA Director. Ellspermann says economic development and innovation will be the administration's focus in agriculture. Sheets is particularly suited for that focus, after most recently serving as the Director of Economic Development and International Trade at ISDA.

# Chapter 10:  Building a College

As I have shared the story of the development of LICC, I have constantly mentioned those who helped. There is a reason for this. We started from nothing, but actively and prayerfully engaged people, working hard to create all the things that make LICC what it is today—a fully accredited college with over 200 students enrolled and 40 faculty and staff, offering four academic disciplines: education, agriculture, theology, and business management.

## The First Building: Classrooms

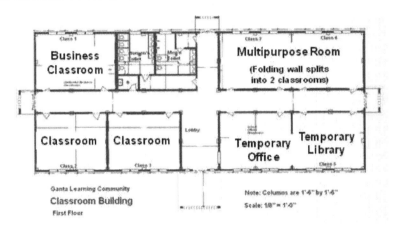

Russ and I scheduled and actively met on Wednesday nights as we brainstormed the design of the first building—the one that would house our classrooms. We discussed how big we wanted the classrooms to be and how I wanted them to be like American-style classrooms, using pictures of various American classrooms as the model.

Once we settled on the model, we designed the first building and began construction of the first floor because that would give us classrooms to start teaching students even if the second floor was not complete yet. Our hope was to eventually complete the second floor so we would have room for offices for our professors and administrative offices.

Once we had a plan, we waited for the opportunity for Liberia to be safe enough to begin building since the civil war was still on and off. When peace was finally established.

The first need was to lay the foundation. Fortunately my good friend Lee Wuanti, a fellow Liberian now living in Elk Rivers, Minnesota, volunteered to go to Liberia to oversee this. Both Lee and his wife Narko were excited to be part of this effort. Preparing the foundation was a much bigger chore than it would be in the developed world. After preparing the earth using only hand tools, and installing the wooden forms that would shape the concrete, we needed concrete. Unlike in the developed world where you buy a truckload of concrete and have it delivered and poured at your site, we had to mix all our own concrete from bags of concrete we bought at various stores. No store had as much concrete mix as we needed. Then wheelbarrow by wheelbarrow, up wooden ramps, we dumped it into the forms. Thanks to all the efforts of local volunteers, and Lee Wuanti, the foundation was completed in May 2006.

Moving Cement Up Ramp in Wheelbarrows

Volunteers from various churches of different denominations in Ganta turned out in large numbers to backfill the foundation by hand. Our next task was to find a contractor to start the building. We found one who seemed reputable, but it always seemed that there was some problem arising that cost us more and more money. We had limited funds, but what we had raised should have been enough for our planned first floor.

Unfortunately, work proceeded slowly at best and often crawled to a stop. Reluctantly we were forced to fire this first contractor and find a new one. After that, we were fortunate to have Grace Church attendee Chris Royston spend three months in Liberia to oversee the building of the first floor classrooms.

God blessed us, and we found a new contractor who worked for 60% less per hour and did more. The new contractor was able to help us with additional work, including electrical work, plastering, laying the floor, and even laying the floor tiles. The only thing we had left was to paint and furnish the building.

We dedicated the first floor of our classroom building on June 14, 2008. It was an exciting time for all of ULICAF. All our hard work and the money we had donated had resulted in a tangible building!

## Fleshing out the Campus Master Plan

A vision is a beautiful thing, but to come to fruition it needs more than a bright smile and flowery words. A vision, when it comes to reality, must address the details. Russ Schwartz had helped us create a conceptual plan. Now it was time to look at more of the details of how we would build our college. What would the whole campus look like when it was complete?

We were fortunate at this time to learn of a group of engineers and architects in Colorado Springs called EMI (Engineering Ministry International) (www.emiusa.org). They took a look at our overall college plan for the 20 acres of land. They listened to what we wanted to do on this land. For example, how many students we would like to serve, the types of buildings we wanted, the majors we would offer, and so forth. We talked about one of our major desires which was to have a worship center on campus. We talked about things we probably would not be able to do any time soon like dormitories. They looked at our conceptual plan and checked it for alignment. Would the buildings we believed we needed (classrooms, learning center, and worship center) meet the needs of our goals? Did our plan and goals align? We found some parts that were not in alignment. Mostly however, we found that our plan made sense.

Then came time for their field work. Once it was approved by their organization, they sent eight engineers over to Liberia to do a detailed topographical survey of the campus and to conduct the essential tests needed in planning such things as future septic systems.

They spent two weeks with us, staying in our renovated guest house in Ganta. This was a house we bought in Ganta and renovated by adding a dining room, bathrooms, and a generator room. Our plan was to use it for short-term missionaries and this fit nicely. We paid the airfare for the team leader, but all the other members of the team paid their own travel expenses and the team leader even paid part of his expenses. On completing the survey, they went back to Colorado and 2–3 months later sent us a CD. It contained a campus master plan which we were able to have printed out on drafting-type paper. This plan took us from a single building to a full campus with multiple buildings! It gave us something to show our donors and prospective donors. The plan included exact dimensions. We have made some modifications as we have gone along, but we began to lay out the campus based on that plan.

The CD also included detailed plans for a second story for the classroom building, an administration building, a library and bookstore and a campus main entrance. Their estimate of cost to build our first three buildings was one million dollars! It was a shocking number to us, but we knew that Liberian construction costs were much lower than U. S. costs—at least we hoped so. As it turned out, the cost estimate was high and we were able to construct our buildings at a lower cost per square foot. It makes sense that costs would be lower, but for a few moments, we had a scary feeling digesting the potential cost.

# The Need for a Guesthouse in Monrovia

The guesthouse in Monrovia was one of the things we knew we needed from the beginning. We knew we would need outside resources, so we looked forward to people visiting from the United States and Europe to help us to build the school as well as to teach our students. Just as it had dawned on us to have American friends help us with the things we could not do ourselves, we knew that they would need accommodation when they arrived. We did not need to provide the luxuries of a great hotel, but we wanted to allow them to rest after the lengthy flight (often 18 to 21 hours with layover). This rest is also needed to prepare for the next leg of the journey to the college. From the airport in Monrovia to LICC is 150 miles of bone-jarring gravel road. It would be quite difficult for our guests to immediately offload and get on the road. So, we desire to have our visiting friends stop in Monrovia before heading to Ganta. Our wonderful guest house gives our visitors to share fellowship and get to know each other before heading out into the field. For safety and for peace of mind, we felt a guest house was a good and necessary thing.

When we started searching for land to build a guesthouse in Monrovia, our ministry partner, United Liberia Inland Church (ULIC), which had a church compound in Monrovia, allowed us to build a guesthouse on the church compound, so there was no cost for the land to build the guest house. Owning and managing the house ourselves also provides us an opportunity to reduce and control the cost of getting our guests from Monrovia to Ganta.

Besides having a place to stay, our guests would need transportation. Our guests, being new to Liberia, might find it difficult to arrange renting a car. When our visitors arrive, we have drivers pick them up at the airport, and later drive them to our campus.

We have developed a reputation for caring for our visitors in a way that our mission partners can trust. We might have limited resources, but we do what we can for our foreign friends who donate their time and talents to help our ministry.

## The Computer Lab

Although it was part of our vision to provide information technology at LICC, we needed someone with the appropriate skills and background to set up and manage the computers. Bob Henninger was that person. When I came to know Bob in Indianapolis, he was already retired from work, and he quickly responded and participated in three mission trips to Liberia.

On his first trip to Liberia, Bob repaired and equipped about 24 computers donated by a friendly Indiana public school. Most of the computers had very limited memory when they arrived and had been setting in our warehouse for months. Bob spent many hours, taking parts from the computers in worst shape to rebuild those that needed minor repairs. Eventually, he was able to create a dozen functional computers, free of viruses and other software problems. Bob had a passion and a vision for repairing computers.

On the second trip, Bob performed work on multiple software applications and programs, and he networked the computers together for the classroom. A student then could print from any of the computers in the room. Also, on this trip Bob taught an entry level computer class, helping the students learn to use the computer programs. For several of the students, this was their first experience with a computer class. They were amazed and thrilled with learning how to use a computer and seeing their documents printed.

Bob Henninger

On the third trip to Liberia, Bob taught Excel™ and PowerPoint™. Bob was trained in engineering, but also had a seminary degree in theology. Even though he came to Liberia to work on computers, he also taught New Testament classes. We know that Bob really enjoys this teaching, and we have heard many good things about him from his students. This has been a win-win situation with Bob getting the chance to make a real difference in peoples' lives, using his computer and biblical training.

## Electricity and Water

When we started LICC, there was very limited access electricity in any of Liberia. The equipment to produce it and the lines to carry it to those who needed it were either destroyed or in such disrepair they did not work. For that matter, the area outside Ganta where our college is located had never had electricity lines to it. It is not like America or Europe where electricity is available almost everywhere.

If we wanted electricity, we had to make our own. Those who could afford it used a small generator to create some electricity for their own consumption. We needed a large generator and when we the cost of one generator, it was about $20,000 plus shipping from America. Fortunately, we were able to find a supplier in Liberia who was able to sell us two generators for $20,000—with no shipping costs. We built a small building near the edge of our campus, and soon we had electricity to our classrooms, all paid for by a generous gift from one of our partners.

Generator Building

Our Generators

Diesel generators are a solution to the need for electricity, but they are not a completely satisfactory solution. The main reason is simple. We can only run them a few hours a day because of the cost of the fuel.

Bob Henninger, our computer volunteer, designed a simple system based on a solar cell to power small items like computers and to recharge items like phones and laptop computers. We are hoping this will allow us to reduce our electricity cost and make it possible for wider use of our computers and other electrically-powered equipment. Eventually, of course, we anticipated the arrival of public electricity. As of 2015, LICC has electricity that has come from Ganta.

Another infrastructure issue was water. There was no public water supply to LICC. There was no running water anywhere in the Ganta area. So, to get water for LICC, we dug a well. To ensure a regular supply, we built a water tower with a pump system and a generator to run the pump. We were blessed when an engineering group from America designed the campus and included the location of a well and water tower. Even though at the time all we had was the first floor classrooms, we built the water tower high enough that it could supply water to both the second floor and the rest of the campus. All this was possible because of the generous donation of Margaret Beach and her family, in honor of their late sister Eleanor May Cermark.

Unfortunately, since this water is from a shallow well, it is not considered potable. A machine-drilled well (at least 250 feet deep) would be required to get water that would be considered potable. So this is an item still on our wish list. For now, we rely on bottled water sold to us by a business in Ganta for drinking water.

Today, if you want a running water supply, you must create it yourself. So, we at LICC, made our own running water. It sounds like a lot of work, but it was necessary if we wanted water. Hopefully, one day city water will be available in Ganta.

## The Second Building: The Community Research Center

The Community Research Center (CRC) has been part of the plan from the beginning, but had to wait until after we completed the classroom building and obtained adequate funding. The building has two floors. The first floor contains a library and a book store while the second floor is designed to house an online learning center and student project rooms. Now, with quality resources—books, reference materials, and the Internet—we can admit more students, offer a full curriculum, and help maintain full accreditation from the Liberia Ministry of Education.

The CRC's contents, equipment, and space will also play an integral role in the LICC's educational outreach to the surrounding community. To achieve our intended goals, we determined we needed an innovative design for our college that provides online library database access. We wanted to hire remote instructors to make more courses available to learners and to foster more research and collaborative learning.

On July 6, 2014, the CRC was Dedicated

The CRC will have been worth the effort if we only accomplish our short-term goals. Our growing library needed a home and the CRC provides it. It also provides even more value now that it has become a public library (the first in Ganta). We have accomplished one of our long-term goals to bless the local community. For example, we look forward to providing more opportunities for people to connect worldwide with researchers in their field via the Internet.

The CRC received funding from many sources. Besides ULICAF members, we received funding from the Liberian government and a German foundation based in Stuttgart, Hilfe fur Bruder International e. V. The opening of the CRC was a significant event for the country.

## Transportation

LICC turned off its generators by 9:00 PM to save on the cost of fuel. The students and faculty went home in the dark when they left our campus. Many of our students do not have enough money for a motorcycle (a car would be out of the question). The LICC campus is about two or three miles from the city center. In the dark, the trip is not altogether safe. Because of this, getting a bus for our students was a priority for us. We knew a bus would help enormously by saving our students the time to walk from home and back (often over an hour each way). However, a bus is quite expensive—a 20-25 seat bus could cost $100,000.

Second Graduating Class with Bus Behind Them

Then we heard that President Ellen Johnson-Sirleaf had planned a visit to Nimba County for Liberia's Independence Day's festivities, and that Ganta was the first stop. We immediately began to talk with our county's leaders to put LICC on the President's list for dedication. We were fortunate! Our request was considered and the President made an historic visit. The President asked, "How can I help?" We told her about our transportation need for students and staff. The President accepted our request and gave us a grant for $100,000 that we used to purchase a bus with 23 seats. We had some money left over and were able to purchase fuel for one whole year with it, and also provide some scholarships for our students.

So now, the President's story is a part of our story, but a story all her own. She has allowed herself to be used by God in creating this blessing. She is part of the bigger story of LICC; she addressed a need. This is what we are looking for as we build LICC. You do not need to repeat the things that others have done. You have your own story to create with LICC. If you become involved with ULICAF and LICC, we will be helping you weave your story, which is the story of your contribution, into the bigger story of LICC. And that story, because it is your story, will be a blessing not only to LICC, but also to you and the many people in your circle. The Apostle Paul talked about running the race. It is God's race and God's triumph, but it is also our own individual races which tend to be more like relays.

## A Soccer Field

We did not need a soccer field to teach students about the Bible, business or computers. So, a soccer field was not a high priority for us. We did not agonize over it at Board meetings. Yet, exercise and athletics can be a good supplement to rigorous academic study. It provides an opportunity to relieve some stress and to bond with your fellow students.

Even though we wanted a soccer field eventually, we did not want to spend much money on it. God had a plan for our soccer field! The local United Nations (UN) mission had a big yellow machine. We call them something different in America: bulldozers or scrapers.

The UN continually builds roads and helps the community in a diverse number of ways. We wondered if they would help us. Their answer could have been no, but it was yes. They brought the big yellow machine over and created a level soccer field for us. We were very thankful.

Soccer Team with Coach Brandon

Developed societies do not appreciate the value of such machines because often so little labor is done by hand. Using big yellow machines is expected. Contractors do not hire dozens of laborers who use shovels and picks and rakes. Instead, you hire a big yellow machine (bulldozer), and in a very short time the job is done.

But for us, this was a huge blessing. Many of the bricks (cement blocks) for our first building were made by hand by our local community and by our students, using sand and cement. It was sometimes difficult to obtain sand and cement. In some cases, we had to go dig sand out of riverbeds. Then, once we had shaped them, we dried them in the sun. Sure, we could have labored to build our own soccer field, but it would have taken hundreds, if not thousands, of hours of labor. And the result still would not have been as good as that produced by the big yellow machine.

To put this in the perspective of our plan for building a college, an opportunity was available for accomplishing a lower priority goal and we took it. The students are glad to have a soccer field. We, as the leaders of LICC, are glad that creating it did not distract us in any measurable way from continuing to build the college.

107

In 2012 we had our first soccer coach. For 4–5 years, while I attended Grace Church in Noblesville, Indiana, a young boy named Brandon kept asking me when he could come to Liberia with me. Finally, Brandon graduated from high school where he has been a soccer player for all four years. That summer, before starting school to become a chef, he was able to take a trip to Liberia. So, we had our first, and so far only, American soccer coach. Brandon coached us when we played ABC University. Although we lost the game, we played our hearts out.

## A Beautiful Campus

Many of us had attended American colleges which gave us an understanding of the importance of making our campus pleasant and attractive. We wanted our campus to appeal to future faculty, students, sponsors, donors, and visitors. We also wanted to reach out to the local community, to be a resource for the local people. Our first goal is to be a functional campus, but our long-range plan is to go beyond that.

So when the opportunity presents itself, we work to beautify our campus. For example, our fountain, located at the center of our campus, is a unique centerpiece and roundabout.

The roundabout at the entrance to the campus helps get people into and from our campus. For those of you who are unfamiliar with roundabouts, it is a common type of intersection in European cities. Instead of traffic lights which start and stop lines of traffic, lanes encircle a round grassy area which could also have plants or a fountain. A car enters the roundabout by going to the right and exits onto any other road at that intersection (including exiting in the opposite direction on the street they came in on). Besides in Europe, roundabouts are very popular in central Indiana where I have spent many years—which just goes to show, you can get the Liberian out of Indiana, but you may not be able to get the Indiana out of the Liberian.

Because of the architecture and beauty of our campus, people in our community have asked to host events and weddings on our site on a number of occasions. Our campus now serves not just the college, but the community as well as we had hoped.

See the photo gallery on our school website for color photos: www.liberiainternationalcc.org

## Medical Clinic

From the beginning we wanted a medical clinic to serve LICC staff and the community. However, we had to be patient. Eventually, the Lord led us to Zaye Zarweah, a registered nurse who helped develop our clinic in one of the classrooms. It consists of a waiting area, a check-in/out desk, and two examining rooms. Despite its small size, the LICC Clinic is a busy place: In the period from March 2013 through January 2014, the LICC Clinic served an average of 72 people per month from a population of 200 students and 38 staff and their families. Eventually, Zaye moved on to start her own private clinic for families, so we began looking for another full-time nurse.

Miss Edwina Wuo, a student we had supported through our One Hour for Christ Scholarship, agreed to come and be our nurse in March 2013. God at work again. One of our scholarship sponsors had provided Edwina a scholarship to study nursing at Cuttington University in Liberia. After she graduated in 2011 with her nursing degree, she came to inquire if ULICAF or LICC had any openings. Unfortunately there were none. I explained we had no strings attached to our sponsorship and that she could go get a job anywhere. She was hired by an NGO (Non-Governmental Organization) in Liberia. About a year later, I was visiting LICC and during the evening hours, I went outside to escape the heat in my room. Edwina's mother came by and I asked her about her daughter. She quickly said that Edwina had come home to visit that weekend. She ran back to the house to inform her that I was in Ganta. In no time Edwina and her mother came running to see me. I mentioned that we at LICC were looking for a nurse. She immediately responded that she was ready to come and serve.

She agreed to leave her current position and come work at LICC as our nurse. I explained we could not, at least initially, pay her what she had been receiving at her current job. She said she was eager to give back by helping us and accepted the position anyway.

Edwina with Eyeglasses Donated to Medical Clinic

A recurring issue in countries like Liberia is access to medical supplies. Consumable medical supplies such as gauze and hand sanitizer, as well as low-end medical equipment, such as stethoscopes and blood pressure machines, have always been in short supply. For example, in many countries, gloves are worn only once and then discarded for sanitary reasons. In Liberia, they are washed and reused.

## Medical Supplies Program

We have launched a medical supplies program by partnering with International Aid and the Links, Incorporated. International Aid is a Christian relief ministry that equips servants worldwide with the tools they depend on to bring healing and restoration to those who desperately need to know the one True Healer. This is done through the distribution of life-saving medicines, hygiene products, nutritional supplements, and reconditioned medical equipment which are donated to hundreds of ministries and humanitarian organizations serving in the areas of greatest need.

The Lord led us to The Links, Incorporated (Bucks County Chapter in Pennsylvania), an international, not-for-profit corporation. The members of The Links, Incorporated are professional women of color who are committed to enriching, sustaining, and ensuring the culture and economic survival of African Americans and other persons of African ancestry. (Read about The Links: http://www.linksinc.org/about.shtml) Through partnership with International Aid, we have been able to purchase medical supplies at a low cost to ship to LICC's clinic. They have become a primary partner of the LICC clinic in providing funds to purchase supplies and essential medications to provide care to the LICC community.

The LICC clinic, out of its abundance of supplies, has been able to supply the Give Them Hope Clinic, Ganta United Methodist Hospital, and the Saclepea, Garplay and Bahn Inland Clinics in Liberia.

There were plans to develop a community health center and expand these services in the future, but in the wake of the recent Ebola crisis and the lack of access to healthcare that came to light, it became apparent that this project needed to begin sooner rather than later. The land is available and plans are being made to break ground and begin construction in 2016 as soon as the funding becomes available.

Why do we need a health facility? The first is that the Ganta community needs another health facility that provides healthcare at an affordable cost. The second is that we could focus on providing health education to the community, especially as Ganta struggles with preventable diseases such as malaria and typhoid fever. We can immediately help eliminate diarrhea or malaria problems which would bless the community as we partner with them.

The leadership of LICC, in the long-term, hopes to offer a pre-nursing or nursing program. Perhaps we could offer the Liberian version of a LPN (Licensed Practical Nurse) program as a starting point. Our students could gain practical experience working in the health center. The community would benefit from having a well-staffed low cost clinic available. Eventually, the clinic self-sustaining from payments by patients from the community. Accreditation requirements for nursing programs are much more stringent than other academic programs, so we will need professionals to help us design and launch this program.

## Agricultural School

The Bible teaches us to wait for God as we plan our projects, but sometimes God moves our projects along quicker than we had expected. His timing is not our timing!

In 2011, Travis and Gina Sheets came to the Sagamore Institute in Indianapolis to attend a summit on African agricultural work. At that time, Gina was serving as the Director of Economic Development for the State of Indiana. She has extensive background in farming. From that meeting, Donald Cassell, a senior fellow of Sagamore Institute called and introduced the Sheets to me. We scheduled our first meeting to explain to the Sheets our vision to develop the Liberia International Christian College, and to establish a school of agriculture.

In our initial meeting we discussed the values and goals of ULICAF. I wanted to hear their passions and interests. We ask ourselves questions like: Do they have a specific focus? Do they have a workable plan? Do they seem like they will be able to execute their plan? It is easy to believe and have an idea, but it takes energy, focus, drive, and creativity to make that idea a reality. Not everyone can do that. To help with this, I like to hear the story of their beginning.

In the case of Gina and Travis, Gina told me what her responsibilities wer in her job for the state government. I saw what she was doing practically to fulfill her life mission. She said to me, "I work in an office, but I love the soil." She and her husband had gone on some short-term mission trips and had helped build churches.

They had had a passion for Africa ever since they met and heard an Ambassador from a country in east Africa. From this meeting, they found they had a passion for helping farmers in east Africa. When they talked to the Ambassador, he mentioned that an election was coming up, one that would likely leave an ugly mark on the psyche of that country because it was likely to be violent. The Ambassador said to them, "I'm sorry, but now is not the right time to go to my country."

For Gina, this was a door closing, but still the passion was there in their lives. What should they do next? They could have given up on their dream. They could have been distracted by other things (the cares of the world), but they were not. God was faithful to them and to us. Hence, they stuck to their dream and eventually had their initial conversation with our contact at the Sagamore Institute. From him they learned about ULICAF.

Gina and Travis Sheets

Satisfied with our initial inquiry, we met for a second time. I took Russ Schwartz and Bob Henninger to meet the Sheets. I bring people with me so they can learn about the potential opportunity and also so they can ask questions based on their expertise. For example, I am not an accountant. If it is a financial matter, then it is helpful to have the input of a financial person. If it is a computer issue, it helps to have the input of a computer person.

At this second meeting, I asked them to give me their basic proposal. I explained I needed something I could share with the Board. I was still on the fence, but Bob became very interested, even excited, which is rare for Bob. He had heard about diversified farming, but had not seen it practiced. To Bob, this was an answer to prayer. On the ground in Liberia, his experience was that the food was not healthy enough. Bob liked to cook his own food.

Bob, together with the Sheets was able to show me the advantages of diversified farming. Bob Henninger gave an example of raising chickens and also having a fish farm. You have to put the chickens somewhere. So, you build the chicken house over the fish pond. You feed the chickens and the waste from the chickens falls into the pond and feeds the fish. Leftover waste from the fish goes into the garden where the crops are grown that the chickens eat. It is all one big cycle.

I was slow to grasp the value of diversified farming. I wanted an agricultural school, but I realized that if traditional African farming cannot feed a household, we would not want to teach that method at our school. I did not know much about diversified farming as it sounded like traditional farming to me. We have practiced traditional farming in Liberia for centuries and probably millennia. The traditional farming has not provided much advantage for the local farmer to feed his family. For our vision for Liberia, we needed commercial machine farming—at least that is what I thought would help a family grow enough food to feed their family and have some left to sell to purchase other items they needed.

So, I asked Travis and Gina to help me understand diversified farming. A diversified farm is one that has several production enterprises or sources of income. The farmer earns an income from a diversity of crops such as fruits, vegetables, row crops, livestock, poultry, and fish.

Further, they explained some of the advantages:

1.  Better use of land, labor, and capital;

    a.  Better land through adoption of crop rotations,

    b.  Steady, nearly year-round employment of farm and family labor, and

    c.  More profitable (consistent) use of equipment.

2.  Less risk due to crop failure and less dependence on market price of one or two products because the farmer is growing many crops and perhaps even some livestock.

3.  The byproducts (waste streams) of the farm are utilized more productively if cattle, poultry, and even fish, are raised along with crop production—what is waste from one species is fertilizer for a crop while the byproducts of the crops can be used to feed the animals.

4.  Regular and quicker return is obtained because there is not just one big harvest, but a series of harvests through most of the year.

5.  Soil erosion can be kept in check as land is kept under cultivation throughout most of the year.

6.  Soil fertility is improved as land is kept under cultivation throughout the year.

7.   Diversified farming is less risky than specialized farming because not all of the farmer's eggs are in one basket (sorry for the idiom, but it was appropriate).

My question (and it may be yours, too) is how does this differ from traditional farming? A traditional farmer in Liberia would usually grow some vegetables to eat, maybe grow some row crops for cash, and possibly raise some animals to eat or sell. On its surface, it does not sound that different from the traditional farming that my father taught me. Now that I know a little more about diversified farming, my answer to that is: It differs in knowledge and technology.

Diversified farming searches out and uses the best technologies available for small scale farming. For example, between harvests, the farmer will work to improve his land by using advanced composting techniques like lasagna composting (alternating layers of compost materials like animal manure, dried leaves, fresh vegetation, etc. are layered directly on the garden and allowed to compost). Greenhouses could be used to start plants and also to lengthen the growing season. Also, only few traditional farmers raise fish, but this is common with diversified farms. Unlike most traditional farmers, some technology is used, although it is typically smaller in scale than the tractors and combines I have seen on corn and soybean farms in the midwestern states of America.

I discussed this opportunity with several ULICAF Board members and we realized that, on many levels, our values were aligned. Our core values regarding things like integrity and accountability were aligned. This was a good sign to us, but their proposal also had to make sense and align with ULICAF's goals.

What makes a good proposal? A good proposal will talk about their passion. A good proposal will talk about core values—if not directly, at least implied. It will talk about their authority for pursuing the project: their experience, their training, and their skills. They do not need a PhD in their area of expertise, but they should have some training or experience that shows they can do what they say they want to do. We also talk about their spiritual life. We are trying at this point to determine if our values will align. We also talk in detail about the project. We want to know why they want to do it and how they plan to do each part. We can refine the proposal later, but the basics must make sense. If they have the basic background or qualifications and they have a passion, these will lead to commitment and that commitment will lead to achievement.

While we were interviewing Travis and Gina, they were also interviewing us. To the first meeting they brought their pastor. For the second meeting we requested a formal proposal which entailed their asking questions of us.

Travis and Gina Sheets had founded a non-profit organization called *Hope in the Harvest Missions International* (HITHM). To the third meeting they brought a member of the HITHM Board to meet face-to-face with us and see if we aligned with their mission's core values and goals.

As part of the vetting process, we visited their farm in Frankfort, Indiana. The Sheets restrict their use of fertilizer. They use compost instead of fertilizer. As we kept talking, it started making more and more sense.

We invited them to make a trip to Liberia to get a look at the ground. On this first visit to LICC in Ganta, they actually started building their compost pile so it would be ready when they returned in a year to build their demonstration farm! As a result of their quick scouting trip to Liberia, the Sheets felt confirmation that they were ready to take diversified farming to Liberia.

They sent us their proposal online. By this time, we knew a lot about them. We read through their proposal and came to believe their core values aligned with ours and that what they wanted to do was within ULICAF's long-term plan. The proposal looked good. It provided a basic foundation that we could refine.

So we met with our Board to review the proposal and we met with our Program Committee. We teleconferenced to get feedback from some other organizations that support ULICAF. The consensus was that Travis and Gina's proposal aligned with what we wanted for an agricultural school. So, we accepted their proposal, tentatively, adding our comments and a request for more information on certain aspects.

The Program Committee prepared a questionnaire to be used as our request for more information. We were feeling good about the project. We talked to them about doing a preliminary visit to Ganta. ULICAF then had a Board teleconference where we reviewed their returned questionnaire to see if we needed any more information. There was general support for the proposal, so after a little more refinement, we agreed to formally move forward with the partnership.

The next step was a Memorandum of Understanding (MOU). At this point we were getting into the legalese. This agreement would be binding between us and them. In this case, Travis and Gina were asking for some property on the college campus to build an agricultural building and a home for themselves. This was something that needed Board approval. The property does not belong to me or others; it belongs to ULICAF.

Their plan was to use funds raised by their organization to build a house and the needed agriculture buildings, move in for 5 years, and teach agricultural classes. After that, they and we would evaluate the situation and decide how to move forward. We clarified these details in the MOU so that we were protected and they were protected. The MOU had to be signed by both our Board and their Board. We all were in full agreement.

The project was commissioned November 10, 2012. We began formally working together to create the farm. We agreed to supply some land and the Sheets agreed to build a house that would include facilities for visiting professors and a demonstration farm.

Travis and Visitors in Front of Greenhouse

They brought their experience and their skills to Liberia in January of 2013. Travis is the founding Dean of our Agricultural School.

Travis and Gina Sheets' organization, Hope in the Harvest Mission International, is making our Agricultural Building possible by partnering with us. It is a major project and was not part of our immediate strategic plan. However, God provided the opportunity for us to work with Travis and his wife and we took it.

The first floor of the three story building was completed in July, 2014. This floor, which is partly underground, is Travis and Gina's home. The second floor will be classrooms and a laboratory. The top floor will have an area for visiting professors who are there for short-term missions.

Travis and his wife have worked hard and are making great personal sacrifices to live in Liberia to teach our students and communities about diversified farming. Both were involved in diversified farming in America and Travis's wife was involved in economic development, so their expertise is far beyond what we could have imagined.

They are building their own home, but also a part of LICC. Since they and their organization are doing their own fund-raising, LICC can concentrate our financial resources on our other buildings.

Even as the building is being completed, Travis and Gina have been very busy. The amount of work that has been accomplished with God's help is astonishing!

- HITHM worked with a nearby Bangladeshi UNMIL station (United Nations Military Station) to clear ground for the Agricultural Education Center and the demonstration farm.

- Livestock housing has been constructed and the school has started raising guinea pigs, rabbits, guinea fowl, heavy-duty dual purpose poultry, laying hens, and pigeons.

- Row crops of corn and beans have been planted and harvested multiple times.

- Fruit trees including Mexican Guava, white pineapples, four other pineapple varieties, bananas (several types), passion fruit, mangoes, figs, and papaya have all been planted and some have produced fruit.

- We have a grape arbor with five varieties.

- Many vegetables have been grown and harvested, ranging from local favorites like bitter ball, cabbage, sweet potato greens, and cassava to international standards like tomatoes, green beans, okra, squash, radishes, onions, three types of sweet potatoes, sweet corn, and peppers.

The Ag School now employs ten people. As if Travis is not busy enough, he arranged off-campus training on hog production.

One of Our Goats

LICC Visiting Faculty Enjoying Fruit

Travis Shows First Grapes

If we had not been open to this opportunity when it was presented, our agricultural school would have waited, probably for several more years. As it is, being open to opportunities and working through our process allowed us to approach our partnership with Hope in the Harvest with confidence. The saying is, *"going is not hard, but staying is the hardest."*

## Agriculture Policy in Liberia

During the second term of President Ellen Sirleaf-Johnson, the Poverty Reduction Strategy to eliminate hunger and create jobs was initiated. The initiative aims to reduce poverty and hunger by implementing sustainability programs, and to support Liberian farmers in increasing and improving food production. Despite the President's call, Liberia's agricultural production is yet to be realized and production is still a significant challenge to the nation. Liberia's two staple food crops are rice and cassava which are grown in almost all of the counties. Liberia's main export crops come from rubber, palm oil, cocoa, and coffee.

So, the LICC Agricultural program addresses a real and immediate need that is recognized at the national level in Liberia. With its fertile soil and agricultural culture, Liberia should be able to grow or raise the majority of its food supply. Since the Civil War, it has not. LICC Agricultural program is designed to teach and encourage sustainable farming by Liberians for Liberians.

# Chapter 11:  Curriculum and Staff

## Creating Our Curriculum

We started by constructing a building, but a college is more than just a building. One thing, of course, it needs is students. Why do students come to a college? It is not because of the building, but because of what they will learn. So while we were working to build a place to learn, we were also developing the curriculum for LICC. For our initial phase, we assumed a basic program of 2 years of study. We knew we could not do everything in the beginning; we needed to focus on two or three main areas we could do well, so we selected education, biblical studies, and business. We also wanted to provide computer training because it would not only help students learn, but also be invaluable to students as Liberia moved into the Information Age and increasingly communicated with the outside world. Eventually, we wanted to be able to add agricultural studies to the program. However, our initial plan was to offer two-year Associate's degrees in each those three areas.

- Business Administration and Accounting: Here we designed a curriculum that would allow students the training to work in office jobs in local companies or to start or expand their own businesses.

- Education: Our initial goal here was a curriculum that would teach a student what they need to know to teach in grade school. We wanted a program that provides the certification necessary for a Liberian school to accept them as a teacher.

- Biblical Studies or Missions: The goal for this area of study was to equip pastors and church leaders to work in the local community as ministers. This curriculum would include in-depth Bible study so that they would know the Bible well, but the training also would include the important element of how to share the gospel, plant churches or pastor existing churches, and provide counseling to those in their churches and communities.

As a Christian college, perhaps, we could have focused just on the Bible. However, as you remember, we had decided early in the process that Liberia, and even the Liberian church, needed more than pastors. Pastors are important, yes, but the church also needs elders and administrative support, and a host of other resources.

We knew we needed businesses to generate income for church members so they could support themselves, their families, and the church; we knew churches would need IT support; we knew skilled and trustworthy people would be needed to manage the money and resources of the churches. All these skills can help build the church. Pastors alone cannot rebuild Liberia or the church. So we felt it could be a shared outcome.

Future pastors could benefit from learning about computers and accounting and being around those who were studying it for a career. Future businessmen could benefit from grounding in the Bible. It could help keep their focus on God as they build their businesses or careers. It would, hopefully, encourage them to give back to the church.

In April of 2012, my friend Russ and I visited the Baptist Bible College and Seminary in Pennsylvania. The President graciously hosted us for three days and made time for us to visit each functional area and learn their best practices. We learned that the Bible was integral to every degree program offered.

In developing curriculum, there could be courses in many different areas. For example, a student studying to be an educator might study psychology, sociology, teaching, basic science, math, public speaking, etc. We knew offering this broad range of subjects would be a challenge. As a small school, we would not have instructors who could specialize solely in specific areas. Instructors would need to be able to teach several areas. However, we did not want to water down any of our courses or curriculum.

So, we needed to be careful in how we designed our curriculum. For each degree, there has to be a logical sequence of classes that build a student's knowledge and expertise.

A set curriculum is important because it provides us the ability to offer consistent, standardized training. Individual professors of each course would have their own interpretations of the material, but the basic building blocks needed to be the same every semester or year so that students, and their future employers, could count on a degree from LICC as meaning the student had been exposed to and had mastered a certain level of knowledge in particular areas.

In our strategic planning meetings, Russ and I talked about the subject of curriculum development for hours, and, as usual, he was insightful. However, we wanted to find someone with a PhD or Master's in Curriculum Development. The Lord brought Dr. Danny Bowen to us and he accepted our request to develop a new and more permanent curriculum. Dr. Bowen was very qualified, having received his PhD from Southern Baptist Theological Seminary in Louisville, KY, with a concentration in higher education. Dr. Bowen spent hours developing our new curriculum, with the goal of our first full catalog being ready in 2015.

Our intent as we developed our curriculum was to be practical. We wanted to focus on what was needed for specific professions. For example, someone who is going to teach in primary school needs to be prepared to teach reading, writing, math, science, and history, so we wanted to make sure they had that exposure at LICC. We wanted our students to be qualified to teach when they left LICC. Our goal was that most students, after graduation, would be able to step right into teaching jobs.

We wanted them to be able to honestly say: "I can teach history. I can teach reading. I can teach writing. I can teach math." We wanted them to be able to teach more than general social studies and the Bible. We want them to be able to say, "I had computer courses. I know how to create presentations in PowerPoint, MS Word, etc. I have used the Internet for research." If we train well-rounded students, they will have the knowledge to make an impact at their schools, and future generations will benefit. Incidentally, this is one of the reasons we are so intent on getting the library and Community Research Center functional. We want all our graduates to have learned how to do basic research and to be functional in the technology available to most of the world.

We also realized from the start that, for many students, LICC would be a stepping stone to other education. By that I mean, we would not be able to offer enough in our two-year degree programs to qualify students for many professions. However, hopefully, we would be able to give them a good start at achieving their ultimate educational goals.

I compare LICC to community colleges in America. These "junior" colleges help prepare students for professions and trades that do not really require a four-year degree. Besides that they help many students complete basic or core courses before they transfer to a more expensive four-year school. So, even if the "junior" colleges do not complete the development of a professional, they facilitate the students' education by making two years of it easier and less expensive to obtain.

At LICC our associate's degrees take three years. The first year is for preparatory courses. Those include writing skills, comprehension, algebra, etc. (In America we would call these remediation, but in Liberia, many of the students never had an opportunity to have quality teaching in these areas.) The second and third year the student focuses more on specialized courses in their area of study to complete their course of study for their degree. One of our challenges is defining our curriculum so that other schools will accept our credits.

Another factor is that for some professions, fewer qualifications are needed in Liberia. For example, I know many American pastors. In America, people who become pastors have completed high school and four years of university, and usually three or four years of seminary. They are very qualified. In Liberia, pastors do not typically have that much education.

Not that they would not like to have it, but less is available and the cost would be too much. When we educate future pastors at LICC, we have to keep this in mind. Their training at LICC may be all the education they get, or may have to serve them for many, many years until they can get further education.

## Finding the Right Staff

Our goal from day one was to find and recruit a "dream team" who would work together to build God's kingdom. But how and where do you find employees with the qualities of a dream team member? Several years ago at a Global Leadership Summit, Bill Hybels, Senior Pastor and founder of Willow Creek Church, shared his own frustration with the hiring process. He talked about how he had tried all different sorts of approaches and systems for finding quality people. And for 20 years the effort was heading nowhere. But the Lord came to his aid, and Bill designed a simple approach called the **"Three C's."** A year ago, I discussed each of these C's in a chapel series I gave at LICC. I then began to use the 3 C's for recruiting and hiring staff at LICC.

The first C stands for **Character**. You must make sure that the person you are about to hire has a proven record of being a truth-teller, a covenant keeper, a person who seeks to be conformed to the image of Christ, and someone who values and manages relationships well.

After the person has passed the character test, the next C is **Competence**. If you are hiring for a teaching position, ensure that you hire the best, most gifted teacher (or as close as you can get). Do everything in your power to seek the best, and wait if you need to until you find the one that is "perfect" for the job. In other words, look for the maximum competence.

The third C is **Chemistry**. Chemistry is for team work. A person must be a great "fit" for the team, work well with others, appreciate others' achievements, and be willing to make sacrifices for the team to be successful.

Like Bill, I too have had frustrations when I hired on the basis of competence and overlooked character and chemistry. In 2013, I hired someone to serve as our Vice President for Academic Affairs. I made it abundantly clear that all my senior staff would live in Ganta and not Monrovia and commute.

First, the road was bad and very dangerous. Second, our senior staff members are expected to give us their maximum strength and energy. They are to be mentors to our students, which would be hard to do if they had to dedicate 4 hours or more a day to commuting. We scheduled a first of the month start date and provided a relocation fund for his move. Instead of reporting on the first of the month, he showed up on the 19th. To add more to my frustration, we had to pay him for the whole month. During the following months there was one excuse after the other as he continued going in and out of Ganta from his home in Monrovia. Finally, at the end of the semester, I was forced to let him go. Although he had all the right degrees to indicate very high competency, there were shortcomings in character and chemistry. We had some hint of concerns early on, but we decided to hire him anyway, partly based on the assumption that people will grow if we bring them in and give them the opportunity. And it is true sometimes people will rise to the challenge. Unfortunately, this does not always work out.

How do we recruit staff? ULICAF started with people we knew had the interest and skills, people in Liberia or Liberians in the United States who were anxious to come home. Also, we found that we were able to get volunteers to come over from America and Europe to help. However, we realized we could not fill all our needs that way—Liberians with Master's level training do not grow on trees. So, when we have needs, we advertise in one of the Liberian newspapers such as *The Inquirer* (theinquirer. com.lr). We ask them to send us their Curriculum Vitae (CV) which is the normal process for a professor applying for a position at a college. If the CV looks promising, we call for an interview. Typically, we have three interviews, and then make our decision. If we hire them, we give them a three-year contract with a 90-day probationary period.

## Faculty Qualifications

Once we had some ideas about what types of degrees we would offer and what curriculum would be needed for those degrees, we could focus on hiring teaching staff who would be able to teach the courses. Currently in Liberia, the government allows someone with a Bachelor's degree to teach classes leading to an Associate's degree. For Bachelor's degree classes, the requirement is that the instructor must have at least a Master's degree. It is a challenge in Liberia to hire qualified faculty with Master's degrees. Right now, we are fortunate that we have some, but we are making a strenuous effort to find and hire more.

## Visiting Faculty

From the beginning we planned to make use of part-time and visiting professors. We knew we were unlikely to be able to afford full-time professors for all our courses. An example of this is when we had four theology professors from California visit for a week to teach theology. This represented a rare and unique opportunity for our Bible scholars to interact with and learn from experts in the Bible and in theology. Although we cannot expect this each semester, we are hopeful that we will have more visitors like that.

## Distance Learning

Another area we hope to pursue as the Internet in Ganta becomes more reliable is distance learning. For example, a professor in the United States could teach a business course in our college from his home or office. This would provide another opportunity for our students to benefit from the expert teaching that is not available to them in Ganta. More and more opportunities are available for distance learning with whole degrees and even Master's degrees being available online, so we will work to find compatible courses and seminars for our students. This can also give opportunities for blended learning where a professor might do part of the course online and then come to the school for a week or two to meet students and do an intensive part or a project.

## Administrative Staff

Besides professors, a college requires many people to keep it functioning—people to run admissions and collect tuition, to work in the library tracking the books and resources, to answer inquiries from prospective students, to assist professors, and to do myriad other tasks. We started with 2–3 staff. By 2013, we had 10 or more including library workers, a nurse, and administrators. Our staffing needs continue to grow.

# Chapter 12:  Our Beginning Students

After the first building was completed in June 2008, we looked forward to accepting students in the Fall of 2008. As often happens, there were delays due to processing government required documents and hiring faculty and staff. So, we had delay our opening, but in March 2009, we began in earnest to teach our students.

## First Wave

Our initial incoming students were not like your typical American college students. Our students were often married and had families. Most were older, in their late 20s or early 30s. They worked at least one full-time job, went to school full-time, and often served in leadership positions at their churches or sometimes had their own ministries.

In most cases, it was not by choice that they had postponed starting college so many years. Often, they were unable to attend because of the war. Or in some cases, students started college, but as the civil war intensified, they had to stop.

Some had had to wait until the civil war was over to graduate from high school so they would be eligible for college. This was for the simple reason that public grade schools and high schools stopped operating. In some areas, the only way to graduate from high school was to go to refugee camps, a less-than-desirable situation. We are thankful that so many relief agencies worked to educate our children. However, I know of few Liberians who went to refugee camps so they could continue their schooling there. If they left their homes and went to refugee camps, it was because their own homes or communities were unsafe or there was no food.

So some young people came out of the civil war ready to go to college since they had completed high school in the refugee camps. Not many were fully prepared for college, however, and not all the refugees were so lucky either. For example, if you were in a refugee camp in Guinea, there was less chance for education. This was mainly because the Guineans are French-speaking and our people speak English. Few know French, so they could not take advantage of the schooling.

Another factor was that before the civil war there were few colleges in places like Nimba County (where LICC is). Those that did exist, like African Bible College, only taught the Bible and a few other courses. Prospective students who were unable to travel for education might dream of further education, but without reasonable opportunity, they had to start working instead. Now with a college in Ganta, what once was an unattainable dream, suddenly became a realistic possibility.

Thus, there was a pent-up demand for education among older students—adults who had had to postpone their education goals. This was a demographic we felt led to serve. We felt God was helping us give them back some of what they had lost during the bad years.

Serving this demographic also allowed us to start by not providing some of the things most colleges must provide students such as housing and food. Our students had housing and were already feeding their families, so meals were not as much of an issue as they could have been. This was good for us, as the goal of being affordable would be hindered if we had had to invest in student housing and a cafeteria. As you can imagine, people like this are very busy. We wanted to create an opportunity to learn as much as possible, in as short a period of time as possible, with as little unnecessary work as possible.

Our First Students

These older young adults were some of our best students. They were eager to learn so they could do better at their work and ministry. Some worked for Non-Governmental Organizations (NGOs). They were making a sacrifice to learn, often having to leave spouses and children at home to have the opportunity to learn. They were active in chapel services and attended classes faithfully, participating enthusiastically.

## Second Wave

In our second class, we began to get more students coming directly or nearly directly from high school. Many classes were a 50/50 mix of older and younger students. This group often did not have jobs or their own family. Some had relatives in the U.S. or Europe who were helping them finance their education, but many needed scholarships or other financial help. Few had jobs or businesses that paid well enough to support their studies.

These younger students of the Second Wave brought a new energy to LICC. Most of them attended chapel regularly. This had a positive effect on our chapel services; they became more lively and vibrant. Their energy was evident throughout their educational experience—even in such a small thing as a more social, lively bus ride from Ganta.

They also became involved with their fellow students. For example they designed and created their own bag for their graduation ceremony. It's like a grocery bag with a logo on the side. We have given some to donors. Our students encourage people to give them as Christmas presents.

Some of the Second Graduating Class with Their Shirts,
Hats, Lanyards, and Bags (see p. 105 for the whole class)

They also made the process of graduating more of a celebration and social event. Our older students finished their studies and quietly moved on. To the younger students, the ceremony was more important as a means of giving them an identity with the school and a way to mark a very positive transition in their lives since most had not married or started families—events that would be cause for celebration and overshadow their educational achievement.

## Third Wave

With the influx of our Third Wave, LICC is becoming more like a normal American campus with mostly younger students. It is more vibrant, but also more noisy. We have had to adapt to these younger students. For example, we have started *requiring* chapel attendance and giving them one credit for it. We find this encourages more of them to attend. We have also introduced our first dress code to help maintain a professional environment conducive to learning.

This Third Wave of students is different from the first two groups in several ways. One of the differences is important because it is very positive. Our older students focused on the here and now of their daily obligations. Our Second Wave students were involved in organizing themselves and forming an identity associated with the school. This Third Wave of students is more interested in what is happening nationally. They are interested in their community, but also in their country. Some of them even maintain an international interest. They listen to the news and use Facebook® when they have the opportunity. They have cell phones.

They have become very active in forming a student government. And in 2013 we had our first School Queen who was chosen by her classmates for her support of her classmates.

Miss Liberia International Christian College 2013

While we expected, and have seen, the demographics of our students trending toward younger people as Liberia returns to normalcy after the turmoil of the civil war, I should make it clear we still have many, many older students. We still have many mothers and fathers attending and we have many older students who are actively working and/or engaged in ministry.

Educational opportunities are opening up in Liberia, even out in places like Nimba County. It's not just LICC anymore, but other colleges are springing up. For example, African Bible College introduced a new community college. Also, the Liberian government has just started a new state community college. So there is a much better chance for students to go from high school directly to college. This is a wonderful time to be a young adult in Liberia.

Through it all, LICC continues to grow. As of this writing in 2015, we have 200 students attending, of which we graduated 35 on July 6, 2014.

## Selecting Students

We are selective in choosing our students. Not everyone who applies is admitted. Our selection process begins with an entrance examination that tests incoming students in skills like English, composition, math, and Bible knowledge. Not all applicants pass that test. A student who passes the entrance exam is invited to submit his or her high school diploma and transcript and letters from his or her pastors and school authorities. The prospective student is also required to submit his or her state-administered examination certificates, sometimes called West African Examination Certificate. After meeting all of these requirements, the prospective student is then asked to go to the bank and make the first 30% or 40% first semester tuition payment and bring the receipt to the admissions office. From there, the students is allowed to register for courses with the help of his or her course advisor. At that time the student is ready to commence his or her education at the college.

LICC may not be a good fit for some students and we know this. We are seeking students who we can expect to value their time at LICC, but who are also likely to be able to complete a course of study and graduate. For this reason, we also look at their commitment. If they start something, will they finish it? Will they stick it out through the tough times?

We are also concerned about non-academic issues as a Christian college. Will a potential student give back to society when he or she graduates or will he or she focus only on his or her own welfare? We look at how the students treat others. Are they concerned about more than just themselves? They may be very knowledge about the Bible, but do they demonstrate love for other people?

From a Biblical perspective, it is impossible to really love God and not have a love and compassion for other people.

> Love the Lord your God with all your heart and with all your soul and with all your mind and with all your strength.' The second is this: 'Love your neighbor as yourself.' There is no commandment greater than these. Mark 12:30-31 (NIV)

## Scholarships

Because most Liberian students have limited financial means, we are always looking for ways to help them. We have been fortunate that a number of Liberians and also our American friends have provided scholarships for our students. We have also helped find funding for students who do not attend our college. For example, one day I got an email from a man who wanted to establish a scholarship in honor of his wife. The scholarship will be for nursing students. Even though ULICAF does not train nurses, we were happy to help in this endeavor. Liberia will benefit from having more nurses. Perhaps one day someone who became a nurse using one of those scholarships will come to work in our clinic or teach in some type of nursing program we will offer.

## Meet Some of Our Students

Now that I've given you an idea of the type of student we serve at LICC, I would like to introduce you to a few of them more personally by telling you their stories.

**Jerry Luogon:** Jerry headed the Nimba County branch of a taxi dispatch service. LICC's low tuition and central location in Ganta allowed Jerry to attend late afternoon classes and still work his job. His studies helped improve his leadership and management skills. Jerry built a highly diverse company of 110 drivers from the Mano, Gio, Via, Kpelle, and Bassa tribes. These tribes were formerly at odds with each other. Jerry now works in the national office of the taxi dispatch service.

**Esther Gbor:** Esther is the Registrar at the Christian Foundation School— a primary school which she and her husband founded. Today the school has 418 students and 15 staff. LICC allowed her to attend locally. She has been able to share what she has learned at LICC with the staff of their school. Esther and her husband are involved in supporting church planting activities. She also is a leader of the Inter-Baptist Women's Conference, attended by 600–700 women a year. Esther said:

> *When our school started growing from elementary to junior high, there were a lot of challenges. I decided I needed to go to school, but I could not leave my family and ministry. When LICC came, it was like an answer to prayer . . . a university at our doorsteps. The courses here—lesson planning, Christian Education, Childhood Education, and Christian Ethics—have changed my mentality towards education and my behavior and have been a real help.*

**<u>Musu Kardami</u>:** Musu is Chair of the Concerned Women Food Factory, a Ganta organization that works for the rights and protection of women. Their factory hires women who could not otherwise find jobs to mill cassava, a starchy root vegetable, into a variety of products such as flour, farina, and starch. Musu says that her education at the LICC has made her a better community leader.

**Kau Valentine,** along with her husband Martin, founded the Full Gospel Foundation Children Home at Ganta. The orphanage and school houses 27 children, who are happy, healthy, and very well loved. Kau is an LICC student, and with her husband they hand-built the orphanage from the ground up.

**Rachel Gbartu:** Rachel is the Principal of Hope Academy for the Nation, a primary school with over 200 students. Some students are "street children" whose tuition is paid by the school. Her major in Christian Education helped her grow academically and spiritually as a Christian. She is now able to teach both secular and Bible courses at Hope Academy.

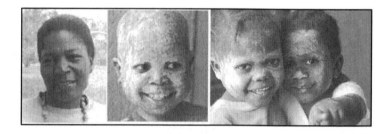

**Mary Ann Newah** works as a supervisor for the Mercy Program at Hope for Nation Liberia. This program takes care of children that lost their mothers at birth, and malnourished children who were abandoned by their parents.

**Reverend John Baryogar:** John grew up in Grand Bassa County but relocated with his family to Monrovia after the 3<sup>rd</sup> grade. He attended public schools in Monrovia and later in Ganta after his family relocated because of the civil war. He received pastoral training starting in high school and became an ordained minister. John has been married to Linda for over 19 years and they have twins as well as some adopted children.

In Reverend Baryogar's own words:

> *My family was a priority, and as I was already an ordained pastor, I found it hard to leave Ganta to pursue further studies. LICC transformed my dream of acquiring a college education into reality. The school provided a good learning atmosphere—a family-like atmosphere, which in no way diminished its academic expectations. There was a strong feeling of anticipation among us students at the time as we were really thirsty for knowledge. My favorite courses were those linked to Theology: I loved Systematic Theology, Missions, and World and Church History. LICC added to my knowledge base and built up my faith; I got to learn a lot of things I did not know and as result, I became confident in ministering the word of God.*
>
> *I am now doing my own research and presenting my ideas in a meaningful way. LICC has taught me not to guess. I would definitely recommend LICC to others because it has the ability to shape leaders. My wife is presently a student there.*
>
> *During our graduation ceremony, the Commissioner for Higher Education in Nimba County stated that if we, the graduates, did not perform well, LICC would remain a Bible College; I did not really know whether he looked down on a 'Bible College' or not. My desire is to see LICC upgraded to a university that would cater to the needs of students from all over Liberia and beyond.*

Presently John is Pastor of the Bethel World Outreach Ministries in Ganta and also coordinates different branches of the ministry in Nimba, Bong, and Lofa Counties. He is active in leadership training and development.

**Pastor Tarus F. Yeanue:** Tarus was born in Nengbein, about five miles from Ganta. His family was large (12 children) and poor. His father died in 1997 leaving the family destitute. To attend high school, Tarus cultivated palm fruits which he sold. He later graduated with a diploma in Theology and Education from Inland Bible College. He returned to Ganta in 2009.

In Pastor Yeanue's own words:

> *I became a student at LICC in 2009 on a work-grant-scholarship, without which it would have been difficult as I could not afford to pay the required tuition to get a college degree. I served as a janitor and was later promoted to head of security, and after a few months I was sent to man the school's guesthouse at Hope Village.*

> *The subjects I loved most were Christian Ethics where I have learnt how to weigh both the positive and negative aspects of ethics; Homiletics which helped me to concentrate on real preaching; Hermeneutics which has helped me to interpret the Bible well; and Writing for the Twenty-First Century which helped develop my writing skills so that I can now write articles fit for publication. In addition, I used to be shy, but LICC changed all of that; we were made to do class presentations and preach during chapel services.*

> *I would like others to experience the transformation I underwent at LICC, so, of course, I would recommend this school to them. I hope that LICC moves from the college to the university level, where Master's Degree programs could be offered.*

Tarus married Avirous in December 2012. He is now the Pastor of the Ganta Christian Church, an inter-denominational church. He also helps out in the community as a teacher of geography, history, and Bible studies.

Special thanks to Senior Pastor Greg Lee and Mission Director David Vineyard of Suncrest Christian Church in St. John, Indiana, who offered scholarships to LICC students. Tarus was one of the three students these scholarships blessed.

# Chapter 13: Our Operating Principles

We had a vision and we created a plan. God blessed our efforts and we were moving forward. However, as we worked our plan, new situations would arise or the normal circumstances of life would occur. The Lord giveth and the Lord taketh away. To guide us through these times, we developed a series of *principles* to serve as guidance. You will hear it told that "the devil is in the details," but our belief is that God operates there as well. We use our principles to guide us in making decisions and dealing with a variety of issues. The great thing about these principles is that they can be applied to many different situations—even ones we did not anticipate when we created our original vision.

We have developed nine guiding principles:

1. Move beyond dependency to ownership.

2. Finish one thing before starting another.

3. Help more than just our students.

4. Take it full circle.

5. When forced to choose, choose character.

6. Avoid debt.

7. Break it into small pieces.

8. Invest in leaders.

9. Resolve conflict biblically.

In the next pages, I will discuss and give examples of these principles that permeate the culture of ULICAF.

## Move Beyond Dependency to Ownership

We, the Liberian refugees who founded ULICAF, wanted the dream of LICC to take us (and many others) beyond dependency. We wanted to develop a sense of ownership among our people.

Sometimes in the West, the efforts of the Westerner do not seem to help Africa improve. The result is donor fatigue. In spite of appearances, the work of the West to help Africa has done much good. Otherwise, many, many people would have died during the various crises on our continent. I am talking about drought, diseases like AIDS or the recent Ebola virus, famine, and people being dislocated by civil war or terrorism. It seems like an endless round of troubles, but the help has allowed people, including many children, to live who would otherwise have died. I would hope we all see that as a good thing. As Christians, we should believe that every human life is precious to God. So, I personally believe in charity and so do the Liberians who support ULICAF.

Let me illustrate. I watched both the 2008 and 2012 presidential elections in America. To my surprise, the two top candidates spoke very little about the poor in America. Instead, the focus was on "Middle Class Americans." I was surprised by this, so after the second election, I asked an American friend for an answer. He explained something very interesting that contained a great deal of wisdom. My friend explained that the focus is on the middle class and not the poor because the poor are always looking for or needing a handout. But, the middle class Americans are dreamers and seekers of opportunities. They are seeking to make a better future and better society in ways that will benefit everyone.

I believe this is why many charity efforts have failed in Africa. There is very little effort to support middle class Africans or young Africans seeking opportunities. You can find charities in Liberia or many other African countries that have been working locally for several decades, maybe even spent millions of dollars, but have very little to show for all those years of effort. Perhaps, we should listen to Jesus when He said that the poor will always be with us (Mark 14:7). It is good to help the poor, but we need more energy put into helping those who will build the future. Perhaps things would have gone in a more positive direction for the countries of Africa if foreign aid was focused more on building local economies and the middle class.

So our plan was to go beyond charity. Our vision was for ownership. We did not simply want to create more charity. We did not want a handout and we did not want to give handouts. We wanted to be self-sustaining. We wanted this to grow from our efforts and continue to produce fruit in others. It is an old adage, but true: *Give a man a fish and you feed him for today; teach a man to fish and you feed him for a lifetime.* We wanted for us and our countrymen to eat for a lifetime. We did know that to build the full college we would need outside help, but our attitude was one of ownership. With God's help, we were responsible for making this happen—and though we would need the help of others, we did not want to be dependent on others for the survival of our dream.

We wanted this for those we would help as well. If someone was hungry, we would help feed him, but our main mission was and is to see them learn to feed themselves. We are teaching our students, and hopefully, this will allow them to provide a better life for themselves and those they care about. We hope our students go on to do many good and great things.

As I mentioned, we knew we would need to raise money outside our community. We knew this from the beginning. So, although it may not seem like much of a difference in practice, we made a choice that made a big difference in our attitude. Think of it this way: Which home do you treat better—the home you own or the home you rent? As a Christian, hopefully, you would be a good steward of both. Even so, there are practical differences. What do I mean? If you own the home, you might invest time and money into building a patio for your family and friends to enjoy. Most people would not do that for a home they are renting. The renters will move on eventually, and the time and money they invested will not go with them or give them any equity.

The lesson of self-sufficiency and independence was first re-enforced in our family by Lily, our daughter. In 1995, when Yah and the children arrived in America, our friends in Holland, Michigan were very excited and extremely generous. Among the many gifts we received were two bikes for the children. Lily and Tonzia already knew how to ride, and took their bikes to school. When they returned, Lily decided that she did not want the bike. Yah and I became furious, and accused her of pride. We made statements like, "Can you just appreciate what people do for you?" But eventually we settled down and listened to her reason. She explained to us that when they took their bikes to school several of the children had bikes, but no one had this type of bike. The bikes they were given were probably about twenty years old, or maybe older. She never saw, not once, the type of bike she had. She apologized for disappointing us, but pledged to work hard and purchase a bike like those her friends had, a bike that she would like riding. In the end, Lily worked with us at a blueberry farm and purchased her first bike from the Wal-Mart store in Holland, MI. These are just a couple of examples of the sacrifices people will make for the opportunity of ownership.

There are many Liberian refugees who have practiced inter-dependency (God and me/us) and made use of the American Dream concept. Unfortunately, there are also thousands of Liberians who live on government food stamps and depend on handouts even though they are able to work. There are also Liberians who genuinely need some relief due to disability; I do not downplay their needs.

## **Finish One Thing Before Starting Another**

Bob's house, our affectionate name for the house for visiting teachers, is an example of how we were guided by our policy that we would not start another project until the project we were working on was complete. Bob was visiting in 2010, setting up our computer lab, teaching computer courses, and teaching theology. He was staying in town, about 3–5 miles away from LICC and getting rides on motorbikes to LICC. Those rides were on dusty roads on the back of motorcycles. It was not the best for

Bob's health, and the effects began to show. Bob came here to help. I knew we needed to do something to make Bob's situation more manageable.

So, I started on plans to build Bob's house. I persuaded the school administration and students to help and we broke ground for the building. We laid the foundation with left-over materials from our previous construction.

When I returned to the States, I brought this to the Board. My argument was that we needed to do this now, because Bob was in Ganta. It could not wait. I shared that we were doing this not just for Bob's sake, but for the sake of the school. Other visiting teachers would face the same kinds of challenges living in Ganta and commuting to LICC. Our Board President insisted we did not have money for it. He reminded me of our principle that we did not start a second project until the first one is finished. We were both passionate in our beliefs. We argued back and forth for hours. The argument at times was heated.

At the end of the discussion, our Board members considered the matter and chose to stick to our principles. I will admit I was not overjoyed. However, I also did not take it personally. It was not a matter of someone being right and someone being wrong. It was about our policy; it was about the way we do things; it was about our principles. This is important for the health of our organization. We can argue, but we do not take it personally. In the end, what matters is that we keep on moving forward.

For me, it was a matter of faith and trust. For us, for ULICAF, it was a matter of moving forward with our plans. We were fortunate; we got a big gift for the project we were working on. That was a happy event for us concerning our current project. And, we did eventually build Bob's house.

That is a story in itself. The students greatly appreciated Bob's help. So we pulled the students together. We said, "He is making a sacrifice for us. By living so far away from the school, as an American, he is taking a risk beyond what he normally would. Let's help him. Let's build Bob's house."

So we invited the students, some of whom did not have the money to pay school fees to help by giving a pack of nails or a bag of cement. I asked our Admissions officer, "Do you think these students can help? Many are already struggling just to pay their tuition." This opportunity taught us something about these students. Not all could help; some were too poor. But those who could help were faithful to their commitment. Having Bob's house has allowed him, and many others, to help us even more than he did before.

Another example of this principle is when we applied for a grant from a group in Grand Rapids, Michigan. We were hoping for help with what was our current building project. If they were only interested in a new building, we had in mind a project we would ask them to sponsor—one of our smaller buildings. For a major building like the Community Research Center, the cost to build it would be higher than what we thought they would or could provide. So we planned to ask for their help with an existing project, or one of the small buildings. Instead of those choices, they suggested they would provide half of the cost of a larger building that we were not working on yet. This is not the way we operate. If they would not provide the full cost of construction, we would have had to raise money for the rest. That would have distracted us from our other activities, like the Research Center. We asked them if they were willing to go the full measure. After discussion, they came to understand our principle and our focus on what we were doing now. They provided a grant for the Community Research Center. We appreciate the help of all those who have given to make LICC possible, but we do not jump on every offer for a new project. First, we make sure we have our current projects under control.

By not taking on more than we can do well at the time, we do not end up stranded and out of money with several half-finished (and fully useless) projects. One finished building that we can use is better than 2, or even 3, that we cannot use! This is because we operate as a faith ministry. We are trusting God to provide for our needs. We do not have the luxury of going to a bank and getting money and doing whatever we want with it. Instead, we try to avoid spreading ourselves too thin—and wait for the Lord to provide. With this type of approach, we have to be carefully how we go about our projects. We create stages of useful results. If we cannot build both floors, we design a building that will be usable with just one floor. That is exactly what we did with our first building of classrooms.

Right now, we have a two-story classroom building that we are using and a library and technology center that we have just moved into and will be using soon. We wanted to finish the library 100% before we moved into the building. We do not want to spread ourselves too thin, because then we will not finish anything. There is a biblical message about this in Luke chapter 14. Jesus talks about figuring out whether you can build before you start. This a message that applies to building projects, but other areas of life as well. At ULICAF, we think this way as we undertake projects:

> *Suppose one of you wants to build a tower. Will not you first sit down and estimate the cost to see if you have enough money to complete it? For if you lay the foundation and are not able to finish it, everyone who sees it will ridicule you, saying, 'this person began to build and was not able to finish.'* Luke 14:28-30 (NIV)

By maintaining discipline on focus, we maintain our integrity. If we start something, we start it intentionally and we strive to do it in a timely manner. If something goes wrong in the middle, we have to work it out and continue on. If challenges become many, frequent, and large, we may slow down. We may not be able to complete the work as fast as we would like, but we keep on working. That is what we do. Our members can count on that.

## Help More Than Just Our Students

As Christians we should love God. If we really love God, we will love others and we will help others.

> *Whoever claims to love God yet hates a brother or sister is a liar. For whoever does not love their brother and sister, whom they*

*have seen, cannot love God, whom they have not seen. And he has given us this command: Anyone who loves God must also love their brother and sister.* 1 John 4:20-21 (NIV)

At LICC, our goal is love (help) not just our students, but also to love (help) the community LICC is located in. For example, our students will benefit from a library and computer lab. That is true. However, the library could also reach out to the community. If that is a guiding principle, then it will affect how we build and maintain our college.

For a library, one area is the choice of books. Our students need books specific to their areas of study, but what is useful to those in the community might be something different. So, if our principle is to help the community, then we need to take that into account as we grow and expand our library.

Let's look at another example regarding the library. Our students can access our library when they are there to study and attend class. Good. That is what the library is for. However, our community may not have the same option for access. Suppose someone works during the day, how will they have access to the library if is only open during the day? Of course, to start out we need to serve the needs of our students with what limited resources we have. But, as the library grows, we would seek to reach out to the larger community and as we do so, it will likely change the way we run our library.

We are responsible to one another and to the community. We take our beliefs seriously because our actions will affect the advancement of the kingdom.

## Take It Full Circle

Every institution succeeds or fails because of its teaching team. The writer of Ephesians describes teachers as God's gift to the Church for character development and ministry preparation (Eph. 4:1).

If good teachers are gifts from God, how could we find the kind of gifted teachers we would need to lead LICC? The best place to start was with our students and graduates. First, we hired the best among our graduates to join our team as staff or faculty, and we encouraged them to eventually obtain advanced training and return.

We have hired some of our first graduates to work with us: Enoch Sayegbouh, Director of the Library; Othello Paye, Teaching Assistant in Theology; Chestin Polay, Director of Procurement; Jackson Zekpeh, Library Assistant; Henrietta Bahrn, Administrative Assistant; and Veronica Yah Wilson, Accountant. Not pictured: Cephas Kolle, Director of Information Technology; Koligar Merklee, Teaching Assistant in Christian Education; and Sam Vannie, Chief of Campus Security.

Enoch Sayegbouh, Othello Paye, Chestin Polay, Jackson Zekpeh,
Henrietta Bahm, Veronica Yah Wilson.
(Also in picture is Peter Mengun, an LICC graduate who was Student Council President,
and is now working for another organization.)

Second, we have established a staff and faculty development scholarship program to upgrade the skills of all our young faculty and staff. The program supports these young staff as they pursue further degrees in higher education. The program also provides ongoing in-service training opportunities for young staff by getting them to do additional course work in their respective areas in the college. We had a short term professor from the U.S. who taught a managerial course that two staff members were able to take to grow their knowledge in this area.

We wanted to create a school where our students could take foundational studies and earn a degree and possibly go on to achieve more education, and then come back and teach at our school if there was a need.

I did not experience this level of support myself. When I went to Bible College in Liberia, the expectation was that I would go back to the villages and preach. Period! Nobody expected me to go further, and we were discouraged from getting further education by the administrator's refusal to give our transcripts to us. In spite of that, I went on to get a Master of Divinity degree at Nairobi Evangelical Graduate School of Theology (NEGST) in Nairobi, and a PhD in Educational Leadership and Policy Studies at Loyola. I believe this further education allowed me to contribute more than if I had simply gone back to local evangelism. In the end, only God knows. However, in helping found LICC, my fellow Liberians and I have helped train future pastors who will go on to help many, many more people.

Taking it full circle also means being able, at times, to help others besides our students and community. In 2013 a group of European visitors came to Ganta. They did not come specifically to see our college, but came to see what was going on in Ganta. The group consisted of about 18 to 20 people. When we heard of this, we loaned them our bus to get around for the 12 days they were in and around Ganta. For one thing, our bus has air conditioning, which is still somewhat rare in Liberia. The Europeans were very thankful for our help. We said, "You are our partners as Christians. We are all advancing God's kingdom." It is good to receive, but it is more blessed to give and we felt blessed to be able help these visitors on their journey.

## When Forced to Choose, Choose Character

Every organization would like its leaders to be fully qualified with recent experience that is relevant to the job they are applying for. However, the perfect job applicant is not always available. So, the organization may need to choose among several applicants who do not meet all the desired attributes. Here is one of our guiding principles: when forced to make a choice, we choose character over qualification. Who would want to be operated on by a surgeon with no qualifications even if he was a wonderful guy? But when faced with two candidates of relatively comparable qualifications, our choice is to choose the one with the most character qualities.

This is not just a spiritual choice but a practical one as well. People with character defects often make bad choices that affect their performance on the job. If someone gambles recklessly, for example, there is the real possibility they may feel compelled to steal if they suffer major losses. If someone is addicted to alcohol, their job performance will often suffer. This goes beyond the performance at work. Unfortunate or overwhelming personal circumstances will rob the person of the time and energy needed to focus on the job he or she is hired to do.

## Avoid Debt

One of our principles is to avoid debt. We make our plans around what we sense God wants us to do. If God provides the resources for those plans, we will implement that part of the plan. If God does not seemingly provide the resources, we will often look for creative ways to do the work or break the work into smaller pieces. If we cannot find a creative solution even for those smaller pieces, we will wait. We avoid advancing by using debt.

It is a Christian principle to believe the Lord will give us the resources we need to do the work He has set before us. As Christians, most of us believe this. This goes all the way back to Abraham, who was ready to sacrifice his son because God had asked for that sacrifice. Remember the words of Abraham in answer to his son's question when they went to make the sacrifice:

> *Isaac spoke up and said to his father Abraham, "Father?" "Yes, my son?" Abraham replied. "The fire and wood are here," Isaac said, "but where is the lamb for the burnt offering?" Abraham answered, "God himself will provide the lamb for the burnt offering, my son." And the two of them went on together.* Genesis 24:7-8 (NIV)

Yet, it often seems the case in our lives that God does not provide, or at least, He does not provide all the things we feel we need or He does not provide them when we want them. This can be particularly troubling when we are involved in a ministry we see as a means of advancing God's Kingdom. I hardly have all the insight on this, but I would like to share two things we have learned regarding debt.

First, we often say we do not have the resources (God has not provided) when what we really should be saying is that we do not have the resources unless we attack the problem creatively and work really, really hard. For example, the students at LICC are helping to build the school. One of the ways they help is by making bricks. It is a simple logic. The students are eager to attend college, but to attend college you must have one. Helping to build the college will complete it quicker so that more students can attend. If we had more money, we would probably just buy the bricks, but because we do not, we try to make do with what we do have.

Rev. Billy Graham once said that God answers prayers in three ways: "Yes", "No," or "Wait." Often God makes us wait for a reason. Knowing that will not take all the sting of waiting away, but it can help us look for what God has for us in our waiting period. One of the most vivid examples in my own life is my time spent in Indianapolis. We went there expecting to return home soon to Liberia to start a college. We had let our own apartment in Illinois go and had packed all our belongings. But circumstances did not allow us to leave for Liberia; instead, we found ourselves in the Indianapolis area. It did not make sense; we felt we were ready to go back. And yet, what a difference the time I spent in Indianapolis made. I would not have met Ray, John, Russ, Ruth, or many other people whose partnering with us made it possible to accomplish this great work that is LICC

Sometimes, like with our stay in Indianapolis, we will come to understand later why God had us wait. Sometimes it never makes sense; we will have to wait until God explains it to us in heaven. Waiting is hard. Waiting takes patience, a thing God must love, as He seems to work so hard to create it in the lives of His children. In the end, the bottom line is that sometimes God does not provide the resources because He has additional preparation or even completely different tasks that He wants us to accomplish before we return to the main work that we believe He has set before us.

## Break It Into Small Pieces

Another way of stating this principle is to start small and grow. In everything we do, we try to break it into phases or parts so that if we cannot do the whole thing (and usually we cannot), we can attain useful results at the end of each phase that, when put together, will result in what had been planned from the beginning. All this, of course, assumes you have a plan! If you do not, you should. This applies not just to organizations, but to individuals as well. We have been fortunate in that we have maintained this discipline throughout our growth. Once you have a plan, you have something that is possible to break into pieces.

For example, regarding fundraising, when we started ULICAF, none of our members were rich and many were struggling to get by each month. We needed to raise money; we needed our members to help, but there were limits on what they could give. We could not go ask our members to donate $5,000 each or even $1,000 each or anything like that.

So we broke it into smaller chunks. We focused on what our members would be able to do. I had learned about SMART goals. That is, goals should be Specific, Measurable, Attainable, Relevant, and Time-sensitive. In the beginning, we were concentrating on attainable! So, we asked for small monthly donations: $20 a month or $50 a month. Unlike a $5,000 check, these money amounts were small enough most our members could write that check—most the time.

And this was our start—the small (or large if you view it like the widow's mite) sacrifices of our members. No one of us alone could build a college; yet, together we could take the first steps required to start the college. Our message could be paraphrased as: "Help us by donating enough to purchase a bag of cement and together we will build a university in Liberia."

From time to time, we would challenge them. If the Lord blesses, please give more. But, if you are on a tight budget, $10 a month is enough. Whatever they gave, we believed God would bless—both ULICAF and the giver.

Just as we asked for small donations from our members in the beginning, we have followed those principles throughout our building of the college. Let me illustrate: We wanted to build two buildings central to the mission of educating our students. We wanted to build a classroom building; we also wanted to build a library/resource center.

Unfortunately, as often happens in life, we did not have the resources on hand to build both buildings. So, we scaled back our plans. We decided we would start with one building—the classrooms. Unfortunately, we did not even have enough resources to build that entire building. At least we did not have the money to build it with two floors, as we had envisioned. So we started with one floor. Our goal was to accomplish enough so that we could do something with what we produced. Once we had a first floor of classrooms, we could start teaching students. Sure, we wanted more rooms so we could teach even more students! We wanted to build that second floor. But, we did "start small" and established a library in one of the classrooms until the Community Research Center could be built. We also wanted a library for the students to study in. But, again, it would have to wait until we had the money to complete it. We could have focused on what we did not have and not moved forward. Instead, we focused on what we did have and what we could do with it. We used the first floor to start teaching students. We got started accomplishing our mission.

Once we had the first floor, we could report to our supporters what we had done. We had pictures to show them that their giving had produced results in Liberia. We showed them that their giving had done some good. We thanked those who helped. We acknowledged them in the book we wrote and that showed we appreciated their generosity. It takes effort and it is a good thing to get a supporter to give one time. We wanted to make sure they valued the experience enough that they would be encouraged to help us with the next project.

We wanted to encourage them, if their resources allowed, to give on an ongoing basis, because our needs did not stop with just one building. We wanted them to be inspired to give again. We have found that our supporters like to hear of our accomplishments and see pictures of buildings and students. They want to know what we have done with their resources. So we shared pictures of the building as it grew and later stories and pictures of the students attending classes. The pictures and stories said to them: This is what your giving is accomplishing.

We continued to work; we continued to raise money. Finally, we did have a second floor. Yes, we had the building we planned originally, even if we had to construct it in pieces. But that was no time to rest. After completing the classroom building, it was time to move onto the library/resource center.

Another way we have been breaking it into pieces is with our tuition. Our goal has always been to keep LICC affordable. For example, housing is available in Ganta, so we did not build student housing because of the extra expense it would create. Similarly, we decided to forgo a school cafeteria where we would feed students three times a day. So we have worked and are stilling working to keep tuition low.

Still, we found some students unable to attend full-time. Sometimes this was because of the cost of tuition; they just did not have the extra money in their budget. Sometimes this was a matter of not having enough time with family obligations and jobs. So we made the decision to remove our flat-rate tuition for each semester and, instead, allow students to pay by the credit hour. We provided options. Students can pay $1,000 a year or $7.50 a credit. We also increased the flexibility on how donors could sponsor students. Maybe a donor could not afford to pay the student's tuition for the whole year, but maybe they could pay part. We believe this flexibility allows a student options that work with God's plan for his or her life. Even if they cannot attend school full-time, they still have the opportunity to pursue an education and learn.

## Invest in Leaders and Empower Them to Lead

We knew that no leader has ever gotten anything extraordinary done by working alone. We knew that to keep the vision going, to keep the college growing, we would need to maintain a supply of earnest, motivated leaders. We also knew that that type of leader is not easily available. If we want them, we may have to take a hand in growing them.

Leaders grow in their abilities with time and experience and learning. Becoming a great leader is not something you do overnight; it takes time to develop character. We have found that education plus practical experience make the difference. If you are trying to develop someone, you need to provide opportunities. Also, from time to time you must provide for their further education. If you are looking to grow, look for a place that will give you experience.

An example of our investing in education is Lawrenso, our Director of Finance, who recently finished studying at Anderson University in Indiana to get his Master's of Business Administration (MBA). He was one of our first key leaders in Liberia. He was doing a good job before he pursued his MBA and we expect that with his training at Anderson, he will do an even better job when he returns.

Lawrenso and Sei at Lawrenso's MBA Graduation

Thanks to the Internet, while he was in America, he was still able to do some work for LICC. He helped with our payroll and created a monthly financial report from the college that is submitted to the ULICAF Financial Committee for review.

We found that if we helped them, potential young leaders would progress more quickly into being able to assume some of the responsibilities of ULICAF. We had several young people who came to our annual meetings when they were students. They came from different cities and states in America, but all showed an interest in wanting to help us. So, we gave them things to do at our annual conference. This gave us a further opportunity to evaluate their abilities to get things done, see what their communication skills were like, and observe how they treated others. If they showed promise, we gave them the chance to lead a section of the conference. After the conference ended, we gave them honest feedback on their performances. If they took this feedback in good spirits, it helped them grow into even better leaders.

Several of these "junior" leaders have grown to the point, through their participation in leadership at the conferences, that they have been able to join our core leadership team. We think this bodes well for the future of ULICAF.

For young Christian leaders, a common thread is learning to talk effectively to others about our faith. Often people feel uncomfortable or incompetent at sharing their faith. Study will help if they feel like they do not have enough knowledge. Comfort often comes from knowing we do not have to do it all. We can rely on God to bring people to us if we begin to pray. When the opportunity arises, we talk to those who show some sign of interest. We just need to do our part. Their salvation is ultimately a choice of their freewill.

As mentors, we can also help them identify their area of competence. When leaders are starting out, they may have a skewed view of what they are capable of accomplishing—or even more common is a skewed idea of what their ideal leadership position would be. Moreover, due to their lack of experience in the world, they may not realize that they have wrongly evaluated their strengths or passions. For example, someone who would make a wonderful theologian might feel that their passion is for pastoring. Similarly, there are those who aspire to teach theology, but whose forte is really reaching out to people on a personal basis. Most leaders are flexible enough to play many different roles. Still, some are great at the administrative part while others are not. Some people make good board treasurers or secretaries, but struggle with leading a committee to accomplish a project. Some people love running a committee, but become bored with staff positions like secretary or treasurer. As mentors, we can help them work through these choices and see where they will likely flourish as a leader.

As mentors we can help the young leader get a vision of what God wants for his life. Of course, we would like them to be focused on ULICAF, but in the end, the leader's time with ULICAF may be only part of that vision, because a vision of a whole life is a puzzle with many pieces. It is not a Bible set in stone. We can talk to them about their own vision. We can talk to them about what they want to do with their lives. Sometimes it will be to become a pastor. Other times, they may want to be a nurse, architect, business leader, etc. We can let them know that they can serve the Lord in those careers as well.

For someone looking for a mentor, I would recommend looking for people who can provide opportunities to experience leadership on some small, beginning level. Even if someone already has the education, they still need the experience. Even someone with a Master's degree may not have confidence or have had ample opportunity for experiences to apply their knowledge. Most of us do not want to fail and that can keep us from stretching ourselves in leadership positions. For those who are over-confident, and there are some potential leaders out there like that, a mentor can provide a guided experience that helps test you, but at the same time provides support if your abilities are inadequate for the job set before you.

That is what we are doing as we develop the next generation of leaders for ULICAF and LICC. As leaders, we can put weight behind our request and get them moving and practicing leadership. If we see they are interested in being a board member, we can invite them to our board or committee meetings so that they can see how we run ULICAF. This mentoring can help them feel comfortable with becoming more involved. As visitors, we introduce them, let them watch us at work, and allow them to ask questions. Of course, they do not get to vote, but they get to participate in everything else we are doing. For us, it is another opportunity to see how the person listens, what kinds of questions he asks, and how he works with others. In this case, it is not just a matter of how he relates to people, but how he interacts with other leaders.

Mentoring has great meaning for me personally. Many of my opportunities for expanded responsibility came from my mentors. Shortly after I was led to Christ my training started. One of my first opportunities was interpreting for the missionary who introduced me to Christ as his team went from village to village. I was helping the missionary, but I was learning as I did it. I watched him, observing how he did things. As I watched how the missionary acted, I began to feel that, with the right training, I could do this too. He was a good and great man, but I began to have faith in myself as well. I began to believe God could use me, too. Later, when I was teaching, he gave me feedback, both positive and negative on the Sunday school lessons I prepared. We would go over the story together; he helped me understand the message in that story. He encouraged me to do more than stand in front of the children telling the story, but to also bring it alive for the children. This type of guided experience provides great learning.

One of my mentors had me give my sermon to him before I went out to preach. This was in the early days of my Christian life. I listened to his feedback, both positive and negative. He would point out areas we needed to work on together. He would say, "Sei, you and I need to work on this area."

For a future leader, an abundance of good mentors may not always be available. In that case, I would recommend that honest and thoughtful peers can make good mentors. A good technique is to seek feedback from people with diverse backgrounds. People who are in different roles see things from their perspective and, taken together, this can yield a better understanding of ourselves. It is like the five blind men and the elephant. Taking the feedback together can yield a lot of insight.

I also recommend workshops, as these can give us a "jumpstart" in a particular focused area. This is a way we help young leaders without spending the money necessary for formal education. Another option for the mentor and for the mentee is being members of a good Bible study. Studying the Bible as a group will allow us to interact with others and receive feedback. Typically, in Bible studies we learn from the leader and we also learn from each other.

We believe it is important for leaders to focus on health and fitness also. A leader will not get very far with his leadership if he is dead! Exercise does not have to be an overwhelming part of life. Perhaps someone goes to the gym three times a week to lift weights and walk on a treadmill; perhaps he runs every morning; perhaps he just goes for regular walks in his neighborhood. We all benefit from keeping our weight down and eating right because this is the only body we have.

A leader should also spend time on himself—most importantly his relationship with God, and then his relationship with his family. This can be harder for a mentor to share than feedback about work, but it can be just as important. A leader needs to be a well-rounded person outside his role. All the things that are important to the average person are important to leaders as well. These are practical things that people need know. If bad things occur in a leader's personal life, they very often spill over into their professional life as well. Sometimes finding time for our personal relationship with God and our relationships with our family are the greatest challenges a leader faces. Leadership is a wonderful calling and it can have joyous moments, but it is much more satisfying if the rest of our lives are functioning well and staying in balance.

## Resolve Conflict Biblically

Conflict is good. Okay, well, I probably will need to clarify that statement a little. Maybe I should restate it that "Conflict can be good." The diversity of voices and ideas of different people can bring great and useful insights. That assumes, of course, that after the discussion, people can reconcile without tearing the vision apart. The vision has to be above the conflict. In ULICAF, you can disagree with our ways, but we do not support people who will work to stop the vision. The vision comes first for us. Many of us have seen how conflict has prevented other groups from achieving their goals. We do not want that strife in our organization.

*Be completely humble and gentle; be patient, bearing with one another in love. Make every effort to keep the unity of the Spirit through the bond of peace.* Ephesians 4:2-3 (NIV)

Our attitude is not universal in African politics. From what I have seen in America and other countries, if two candidates run for a position, the one who loses usually does so graciously. They may not be an active supporter of the winner, but they do not violently work to overthrow their country's government either. This is becoming more common in Africa, as countries get use to the practicalities of elections and politics. It becomes more like two competitors playing basketball. They fight hard on the court, but at the end shake hands. It was not always that way. In Liberia, we had a long and nasty civil war that proved that.

So I remain committed to the vision and to sharing it. We need our leaders to be so committed to the vision that they will work through their conflicts. Our end goal needs to be the same: a college that trains Liberians for a better future. We need to keep in mind the big picture—that this is about more than us: this is for Liberia and it must honor our Lord.

Another of the things we do when there is conflict is to admit there is conflict. We acknowledge what is happening so that we can address it. Someone may say, "We disagree on this, so help me understand your position." And then we listen and try to understand the other viewpoints.

When we see conflict in other organizations, ones that are struggling, we often see that they will not listen to each other's point of view. People get the idea they are right and the other person is wrong. So, they feel that since they are always right (or at least right in this argument) and aligned with God, they do not need to compromise. When pressed to work the difference out, they use their self-righteousness to avoid compromise. Often they feel they would be wrong to compromise. Yet they may be completely at odds with other God-fearing people who hold a different viewpoint! Perhaps someone is right about everything all the time, but that usually is not the case. We need to hold to the truth and our principles, but we need to also remember what the Bible says in Proverbs:

> *A person may think their own ways are right, but the LORD weighs the heart.* Prov. 21:2 (NIV)

There are times when a matter of principle requires we make a strong stand and fight to the last to defend it. At that time, compromise is not an option; we have to stand firm in our beliefs. A good example is our "core values" from which we will never depart. However, most the time we all bring a little truth to the discussion, so considering the viewpoints of others is both useful and helpful.

I have been told that "ego" can be an acronym for "edging God out." If we look closely at these situations, most the time the biggest problem is people's ego. The ego is the number one thing that can get in the way. There can be a solution that will work for both parties, but if someone *has* to be right, he will not even see it—no matter how it is explained. This can be particularly hard on a leader, because, you want your word to be good guidance at all times. He may think that is why he is the leader, because he understands best what needs to be done. To be considered wrong can represent a humiliation, not only personal, but in the leader's relationships. Perhaps, the leader may feel the organization will no longer think he is fit to be their leader—because he was wrong in a situation.

Let me give an example of conflict with someone who has been very close to me and who has supported us for many years.

First the circumstances: ULICAF was sponsoring a student at Liberty University in Lynchburg, Virginia, as part of our faculty development program. At the time, we had given scholarships to three students.

Our Treasurer received an email on Dec. 4. For the next semester, our student would need $6,600 for tuition and $3,000 for living expenses. We let the Board know this. I wrote an email to the board asking for $9,300. It would do no good to pay for the student's tuition if we did not pay the living expenses. Even if financially we might be obligated for tuition only, this does not work practically—if a student has no food and no housing, he cannot be a student. The student could not fast the whole semester and needed some place to stay.

The University called and said our student was registered for the next semester, but needed to verify the money would be paid soon. So we talked about it, prayed about it, and waited to see what God would do.

We had had previous gifts to our scholarship fund. However, the fund was low at that point. Fortunately, a donor stepped in and gave generously to support scholarships, specifically including our Liberty student. I was joyful. Part of the money could go for his tuition; part of the money could go for his living expenses. The donation was more than enough to cover those expenses. However, our Treasurer was concerned about whether the donation could be used for living expenses. Designated funds must be used for their intended use. This issue needed to be resolved, so we had an emergency Board meeting. We settled down and talked the issue through.

I did not want this to be an issue of right or wrong. We were not in a battle for power; we were trying to resolve an issue without compromising our organization or our relationship. Our friendship and collegial working relationship were important. I was reminded from a Bible study I had attended recently:

> *Understanding is a fountain of life to those who have it, but folly brings punishment to fools.* Proverbs 16:22 (NIV)

The tension was high between the Treasurer and me. This had never before happened between us. I asked myself, "What is going on in Ruth's mind? Why did she view this situation this way?" To resolve the issue—to make sure our relationship was healed—I wanted to meet with her. I wanted to communicate that this was not something I was taking personally. I wanted to make sure we understood each other.

From my perspective, I was taking the donation broadly. They had donated to help students. A student has to eat and have somewhere to live. I would have hated going back to the donor who had contributed to cover tuition and say "Sorry, thanks for the tuition money, but we were not able to raise money for food and housing, so that money you gave is lost." I felt we were walking a fine line between rigid rules that fulfill the letter and a looser interpretation that honors the spirit. I felt most donors would consider the intent more important than the letter.

From our Treasurer's perspective, if the donor did not want any of their money used on living expenses, and we spent it that way anyway, we would lose credibility with the donor. This would be a bad precedent to set and might tarnish our good name with our donors. There might also be legal ramifications. Many of our donors are our friends, but they still need accountability and good records. It is always better to be extremely careful to fulfill our commitments than to lose our good reputation.

As I mentioned, this was a very tense discussion. But for our long friendship, I do not know how it would have ended. Fortunately, Ruth contacted the donor and found they were fine with spending some of their donation to help with living expenses. Also, we received additional donations that could be used for this purpose.

When I look at this situation and wonder how I could have handled it better, I came to this conclusion. The perspective of the leader can be different from those in functional roles. It is important for the leader to understand the mindset of the functional person. No one can do it all! I need the help of many people to do my job. I do not have the time, nor do I want to record every financial transaction and prepare year-end paperwork and financial reports. This particularly applies for volunteer positions where the person is helping the organization with no personal benefit and often at personal sacrifice.

As a result of this conflict, the ULICAF Board decided to have a committee look at the issue of scholarships. We made this an opportunity to define how to address this issue in the future. We appointed a Board member as the director of this committee. There is now a Scholarship Committee that receives all sponsorship requests, makes the appropriate decision, gives approval, and informs the Treasurer to make disbursement.

# Chapter 14: Hope is on the Horizon for Liberia

## Turning from the Civil War

From 1980 through 2005, Liberia was a nation of despair. Democracy, good governance, and respect for human dignity were only a distant dream. Today, Liberia is turning around. The era of war and destruction has past, and a new era of democracy is here, and hopefully, here to stay. Liberians have seized the opportunity to build a new Liberia where there is real peace, economic growth, and the hope for lasting prosperity. In this new Liberia, Liberians want, and are working to build, a nation with an accountable government that is peaceful and democratic. We want a country where there is rule of law and there are employment opportunities for all Liberians. Since the 2005 election, more children have returned to school with more girls in school than ever before, basic health services are being made available, and the infrastructure is being rebuilt—including roads that are under construction. More importantly, despair is being replaced by hope—hope that people can live in peace with one another, and that people can have true freedom of speech—without imprisonment. The future of Liberia is now in the hands of Liberians. I believe skillful leaders will emerge and mature and that they will be able to lead Liberia effectively.

As you probably know by now, I am particularly passionate about education, and believe that education is the building block of a strong nation. There are really few things more important for a nation than to invest in its people. With respect to education, the increases in school enrollment and completion rates, especially for girls, in Liberia are good first steps. Last year, when we received our government subsidy, we offered a 75% tuition discount to all our female students.

Other signs of growth and prosperity are the increased distribution of electricity and technology (cell phones, Internet). Today almost every person carries a cell phone. The price of a cell phone has dropped from $150.00 to $12.00. Equally, electricity is becoming available throughout the country, not only in Monrovia like in the past, but in various other counties as well. Our campus now has electricity, along with much of the city of Ganta.

So, although it was a terrible civil war, I have hope. It is true my greatest hope is of a better place, a place where the peace of the Lamb dwells—heaven. However, I have hope for a measure of that peace here on earth. I have hope of seeing God's kingdom spread and grow on this earth. And I have hope for my country.

Liberia is not the only country to have experienced civil war. Many other countries, including the United States, Great Britain, Russia, France, Rwanda, and Uganda have had civil wars. Like most civil wars, our civil war was horribly violent and bitter. Many, many people died. Yet, we know that God can bring good out of even the worst evil. He is always working to heal. He has done that in other countries and we hope that He will continue to work that great miracle among us in Liberia.

We know that God was not the cause of evil. He is, by his nature, good. God created all men and loves all men. Man, on the other hand, is fallen. Man is capable of great hate. Man is capable of de-humanizing groups of his fellowman, and, then, man is capable of inflicting great horrors on those he has marginalized. Yes, we humans can come to hate each other, another of God's creations quite readily. There was much hatred in Liberia before and during the civil war.

I wonder if, from God's perspective, the civil war was also something that could cleanse our country of the hatred among the different tribes and also between the Americo-Liberians and the indigenous peoples. Maybe there is a silver lining if we could lay hold of it. Maybe there is a blessing from God in this great, great tragedy. It may be that only by letting us nearly destroy ourselves was God able to bring us to the realization of our own baseness with enough conviction that we would change.

Maybe now can we look at people of other tribes and of other classes and not judge them on whether they are from a "good" tribe (however that is defined for us). Maybe now we can come to respect the right of all men and women to exist and to experience life, liberty, and the pursuit of happiness—even those we may not personally like. Maybe only now will we have the courage and fortitude to move our country forward in a direction that benefits all Liberians, and not just one group at the expense of the others.

Freedom often comes at a heavy price. For most people to obtain or maintain freedom, they must fight for it. It is through their sacrifice, sometimes their blood, that redemption comes. By their sacrifice, they help build their nation.

Do not get me wrong. I lost my father to this war. I wish it had never occurred. But God is capable of bringing good from the worst evil. God tries to work, even with the framework of our corrupt desires and questionable behavior. What I am saying is that, if we remember the past, we can help protect our future. This past civil war may prevent another civil war from ever happening. Its effects were widespread (everyone in Liberia was affected in some way). It was so horrible. Maybe, just maybe, it will keep us from ever going that far again. Many are committed to never seeing something like this happen again in our lifetime. I am one of them.

In 2012, my friend Donald Cassell, a senior fellow at Sagamore Institute in Indianapolis, made a professional visit to Liberia. On his return, I asked Donald, "How were conditions in Liberia?"

Donald replied with great confidence, "Attitudes in Liberia have changed for the better." Donald is a deep thinker and his choice of words is often profound. He did not just leave it at that. He went on to give an example. The Roberts International Airport, like other important parts of the infrastructure in Liberia, had been damaged during the civil war, but its reconstruction was in progress. Finally, he gave another excellent example to sum up his observation. He noted that people have become unabashedly friendly, and even at times, perhaps too friendly, with a much greater sense of security, purpose, and hope.

## National Issues

As part of this change in attitude, two critical national issues are under public debate. The first issue is addressing Dual Citizenship. Before the civil war, this was not much of an issue, because very few Liberians had the opportunity to obtain citizenship from other countries. Post-civil war, the situation is different. Many Liberians who sought refuge outside of Liberia during the war, and are now returning, have obtained citizenship from their countries of refuge. This also affects many children born outside of Liberia who are returning with their parents. The current law creates a situation of involuntary loss of birth nationality when a Liberian becomes a citizen of another country, without court proceedings or effective due process of law. I think there is a general expectation that dual-citizenship will be written into law, although that may take a change in our constitution.

The second issue is the Negro clause in the Liberian Constitution that permits only persons of African descent to become citizens of the Republic of Liberia. Some of the returning refugees have children of mixed race. If their children return with them, will they be allowed citizenship? Practically, I think the general expectation is yes, they will be considered citizens. However, it may take time for this to be written into law.

Liberia is changing and growing. There was great trauma, but we are moving past it. What did we "gain" from the pain and horror? What can we learn from the civil war? Let me list a few things.

## It Takes Everyone to be a Nation

First, we have a better understanding that we *need* each other. Many circumstances contributed to the civil war, but one of the main reasons for the civil war was the marginalization of a large number of Liberians.

Before the civil war, the resources were concentrated with the Americo-Liberians. Monrovia and certain other areas were developed, but most other areas were undeveloped completely or greatly underdeveloped. Human "salvation" to this problem did not make anything better. A different group was favored, but all suffered in the war.

Because of the civil war, the Americo-Liberians now know they cannot rule without the help of the indigenous people who first settled the land. The indigenous people know they need the Americo-Liberians. If there will be peace, it must involve the entire nation. If you were to go to Liberia now, you would see that even in the Congress there is a mix of people—both the Senate and the House of Representatives. You would see indigenous people as well as Americo-Liberians. You would see a government that is much closer to really representing their people. In realizing this, LICC also has sought to mirror Liberia's diversity in our faculty, staff, and student body.

## Better Distribution of the Resources

One of the other opportunities that has come to Liberia has been the chance to re-create ourselves and our nation. When you start from the bottom, the only way to go is up! However, it is more than that. We have choices. This time around, there can be a better distribution of resources to develop more than the capital city. We have the opportunity to work on developing the whole nation. This is being encouraged and the government is being held accountable by people all throughout the nation being involved. Investment is returning to Liberia, over $19 billion in investments have come to our country. This time it can be distributed more equally for expanding and improving the infrastructure and for social and business development. And hopefully this will continue.

As an example of this, President Johnson-Sirleaf introduced a social development fund early in her administration. Under the President's new law or executive order, all corporations must directly provide specified amounts of funding to help with the development in their local areas where they operate. For example, Mittal Steel Corporation obtains iron from its Nimba Mountain operation in Nimba County. Because of this, Mittal is required to give $1.5 million each year towards Nimba County's development. The Nimba Mountain operation started far back in 1963, but until now, not even a mile of road was paved. Sadly, one hundred percent of the benefits went to the federal government. Not anymore! Now some must be invested locally.

Secondly, each corporation is required to provide scholarships directly to young people and train them as the next generation of leaders. In February 2014, when I reported to work at LICC campus, I was surprised by a long line of primary and secondary students waiting for their registration. When I asked what was going on, someone explained to me that one of the BHP Billiton managers had selected the LICC campus as the place to screen their scholarship recipients. These are just two examples of how the wealth of the nation is being distributed. I think there is more to come as we move toward the development of the whole nation.

Distribution of power is leading to more development. The Vice President (Joseph Bokai) of the nation is from a different county (Lofa County) than Monrovia. Because of this, for the first time, the roads of the capital of *his* county were paved.

In a representative government, there is still greed, but the broadening of the representation helps to ensure that the largess is distributed more evenly. When the government was under the control of just a few people, and their friends, they were the only ones who benefited.

## Gaining a New Perspective

Many Liberians have gotten used to the idea that they have a right to have a voice in their society. This might sound a little strange to a Westerner, but for many Liberians this is a change. Part of this new ideal is participating in democracy and seeing indigenous people being elected and helping to govern Liberia. Part of this is the growing belief that we, as individuals, have the right to free speech—to express our opinions without worrying about retaliation for criticizing the government—just like many other democratic countries.

This belief that we are free to express ourselves is more than just talk. It creates a feeling of empowerment in a general sense. Liberians have begun to believe that we can make a difference in our society by our actions. It's not just the political leaders that matter. We do have a say. This belief energizes us. Of course, to have a good effect, the energy and the right of free speech need to be used constructively. If we, as Liberians, do nothing but complain or criticize instead of taking positive action where we are able, little good will result.

The empowerment extends beyond idle talk. It is the belief that we, the people of Liberia, have the ability to shape the society we live in. We can agree to deliberately turn away from war as a way of solving problems. We can look towards the future. We can choose to make a difference in our country.

## Protecting the Gift

Let me tell you a story that explains what I mean. George DeJong has served as the Senior Pastor of Holland Heights Christian Reformed Church in Holland, Michigan, since the summer of 1990. In 1998 while walking in the footsteps of his Rabbi, Jesus, in Israel, God ignited a great passion in George. Since then George has been committed to a deep study of the Bible in its Jewish context. To "sit under the fig tree" with George in the lands of the Bible is a life-changing experience which I am fortunate to have had.

It was in 2012 that George gave me a most gracious invitation. He paid all my expenses to travel with him to the Middle East. The trip lasted ten days and took us through Jordan, Egypt, and Israel. We flew out of O'Hare Airport in Chicago, had a stopover in Turkey, and finally landed in Cairo.

In Cairo, we boarded a luxurious coach which was our transportation to Israel and for the rest of trip.

From the time we entered the border of Israel to the time we entered Jerusalem, I was speechless. I was shocked at how militarized Israel was. I saw young soldiers that one could easily categorize as "child soldiers" visible in the streets everywhere. No country I had visited or even heard about in my life time was so militarized. Literally, there were soldiers in uniform all over the streets of Jerusalem. We would take just a few steps, and we would be stopped by a security officer to inspect our travel documents. As this went on day and night, I became more furious and angry and confused.

I became angry with a government that has deprived these young people of the joys of youth. Also, I felt the government was exposing these young soldiers to too much violence. I became angrier and angrier. Finally, I realized I needed to calm down and seek a better understanding. So instead of continuing in my anger, one night I resolved to seek the Lord in this matter. Before sleeping, I read from the Psalms (Psalms 43:3) and asked the Lord for an explanation.

Quite to my surprise, I was awakened late that night and was unable to go back to sleep. When I checked the time, it was about 3:00 am. Shortly after, I heard from the Lord, "Sei, what have I given you that is worth protecting? I promised this land to Israel and asked their fathers and every generation to drive out their enemies and protect it." Although I have read this many times in scripture, it was hammered home that night about the gift of the "Promised Land." The land was "God's Gift," but it was Israel's responsibility to drive out its enemies and protect it. It would take all of Israel to keep the enemies out, even these young soldiers. For even today, Israel cannot let down its guard. They must be vigilant if they maintain their freedom and protect their nation and their people.

As I reflected more on this scenario, I began to wonder why so many nations, including Liberia, have been so irresponsible with their national gift. Also, I reflected on how we, as Christians, have sometimes failed to protect our gift—the gift of salvation through Christ. When all of the Liberians failed to develop and protect their nation, we descended into chaos and the senseless destruction of the Liberian Civil War. If Israelis do not take care of Israel, their enemies will drive the Jews out and take over their land. I wish all of us could be like Israel in that sense. I wish that we all valued God's gifts to us with that level of commitment. I believe God's gift to me that is worth protecting is my faith (salvation) in Christ Jesus. I believe the new Liberia is awakening to the reality that Liberia is their "National Gift" from God, it is worth protecting, and it is the responsibility of all Liberians to help protect it.

## Scattered People Bring New Resources

The civil war created a lot of refugees. This Liberian diaspora took them into many different countries. It was hard on many of the refugees, but many gained from the experience. Many of those who left had increased opportunities for education, for example. The result is that those who left have formed a new educated group. In their new countries, they gained skills and experience. They also gained a new perspective on life by experiencing another culture. When they return to Liberia, those who once were refugees can bring the skills they learned back to their adopted country and help develop the economy of the country.

Even if refugees do not return, they are often able to help those who remained in Liberia by providing money or educational opportunities. This can have an effect, even on the local level. There are new houses going up in Liberia, beautiful houses built by the people who are living in Liberia. Some are being helped by those who left. There are children going to school because they can be sponsored by those who left. Yah and I have helped sponsor several students. ULICAF donors are helping six students become trained to be nurses. All of these things are helping to bolster the confidence of our people.

Seeing how other countries work has helped us envision a new Liberia. If they can do it, we can do it! It is a choice we can make. We can emulate the best parts and make our country great, too. So there is a new Liberia rising from the ashes of our near destruction. We are not the only country to experience this.

One example of rising from the ashes is Ghana. In the 1970s, Ghana was faced with a very tough economic downturn. Its citizens were desperate and poor, and that led them to scatter all over the world, including even to Liberia! At the time, it was better in Liberia than Ghana for many individuals. Many Ghanaians became teachers in other countries. Eventually, the economy improved a little, and people started to return. To help those who returned, President Jerry Rawlings made a decisive move by passing a law. Large businesses could no longer sell in retail stores. They could only sell wholesale goods. They were given three years of tax exempt status to make this transition. This was so Ghanaians who returned could have a place to start. The returning Ghanaians created small retail businesses. Today, in Ghana, a democracy has developed like the one in America.

Not too long ago, a Ghanaian President suddenly died of natural causes while in office. His Vice President took over, followed by an election. There was not a coup; there was not a violent uprising. There was a smooth transition in power, a transition that benefited Ghana and all Ghanaians. We hope to see the same types of transitions in Liberia.

Some of the successful Ghanaians, like Roland Agambire who built a business empire, use part of their wealth to give back to their communities. Because Roland climbed the ladder of success himself, he is not just sitting back and looking down on the less fortunate, but he is helping some of them to get their own start in life.

There are other examples in Africa as well. For decades most of the population of South Africa suffered under the system of Apartheid. To have a chance for a future, many black South Africans had to leave South

Africa altogether. Apartheid was not defeated overnight. It took time; it took decades of effort by many people. It took the outside world's condemnation. Yet, in the end, Apartheid fell. And today, opportunity and wealth is spread more widely than ever before in that country. Is it without problems? No, it is not, but the debilitating system of Apartheid has fallen, and all men and women are now equal—not just in God's eyes, but in the eyes of the law as well.

## The Material Fruits of Peace are Arriving

Already the fruits of peace are being seen in Liberia. At LICC we struggled with an electrical generator and a few hours a day of electricity, difficult travel because of bad roads, and lack of fast internet service. In July 2013, electrical service came to Ganta, and the President came to Nimba and commemorated this event. And, as I write, they are paving the road from Monrovia to Ganta and then to the Ivory Coast. Yes, the material fruits of peace are arriving. However, if the blessings are to continue and if our children and our children's children are going to see the blessings of peace and prosperity, our hearts must remain in the right place.

In January, 2014, I took four Americans with me to be short-term teaching professors. Prior to ending our stay in Liberia, I invited three of our teaching professors to visit Malachi Matthew, one of our LICC's graduates in Buchanan, the capital of Grand Bassa County. Buchanan is a coastal city about 47 miles from Monrovia. The road is one of the first highways outside Monrovia to be paved in post-war Liberia. The Chinese paved the road and did beautiful work. It is now one of our first expressways in Liberia!

Another road that is currently under construction is the Monrovia-Ganta highway. We are eagerly, but patiently, awaiting the completion of the 150 miles of Monrovia-Ganta highway, and the comfortable rides that will be afforded to travelers, especially since all who come from outside Liberia to help or teach at LICC travel this route.

We felt education was important from the beginning. Let me expand a little on this. With all this development coming to Liberia, it becomes a question of who will do the work. The electrical work and the road work require money, lots of money, but they also require workers. Who will build the road? The yellow machine will not run itself; who will run it? Who runs the generator? Who puts up the wires to run electricity to individual homes and businesses? The answer long-term, even if it cannot be short-term, should be Liberians. If Liberia is going to fully benefit from all the development money pouring into Liberia, then Liberians need to do as much of the work as possible. Here, again, we see the benefits of education and how it is necessary to develop a skilled workforce.

We do not want Liberians looking for handouts; we want Liberians looking for opportunities. If all of Liberia is looking for a handout or looking for financial aid, we will not prosper as a nation. Teach a man to fish and he can eat for a lifetime.

## Peace is Being Realized

As Liberia is being restored, peace is also felt in and around the country. Liberians are beginning to grasp that peaceful relations, reconciliation, and rebuilding or building the country's infrastructure are indispensable to their new democracy. Liberians are embracing and participating in good government. The Liberian post-war government is allowing freedom of speech and so far there are absolutely no political prisoners held in any part of Liberia. Myriad instances of misruling and bad governing are being replaced by good and responsible governing which is a positive step toward creating a foundation for a better future. This commitment to the rule of fair and democratic law, both by the people and their government, makes a strong case for making a peaceful and stable Liberia that is poised for a flourishing economy and improved welfare of the populous.

For example, LICC was recently (recently to this writing) visited by UN troops. We wondered what this could be about! Being visited by representatives of an army has not always been a good thing in Liberia.

This was different. The representatives were going from institution to institution to see if anyone was being threatened. They asked us if we were having any troubles. We honestly and gratefully could say "no."

It is a different Liberia and we are blessed because of it. We must continue on our current course and never again let hatred and misunderstanding drive our country to civil war.

# Chapter 15: What is Next for LICC?

With the graduation of a third class, the dream that had been LICC became a reality. We had been able to accomplish what we had set out to do. We were helping to rebuild Liberia and strengthen the church. And we were very much on track.

Maybe I should add a clarification: we were able to accomplish what we had set out to do in the first phases of our plan for LICC. However, building LICC does not stop here, nor does ULICAF's mission. The next steps include focus in the following key areas.

## Make LICC Sustainable

One of my main focuses (as of this writing) is to make LICC sustainable. We have proven that, with God's help, we can build a college or a university. We have shown that, with God's help, we can develop a curriculum and assemble a faculty. We have trained and graduated students. However, it is not enough to train one or several classes. LICC needs to be on a sure footing so that it can last for decades.

I have been fascinated by the growth and expansion of Nairobi Evangelical Graduate School of Theology (NEGST). I entered NEGST in 1989 to pursue a master's of divinity.

Dr. Byang Kato of Nigeria was concerned that Evangelical Churches in Africa were providing substandard theological training for their pastors, and ultimately, that would lead to syncretism in African Christianity. Thus, there was the need for graduate level training as a means of equipping biblical theologians to provide leadership for the Church in Africa.

Tragically, in 1975, Dr. Kato died in a swimming accident in Kenya before the school could become a reality. Thereafter, the Association of Evangelicals in Africa and Madagascar took the responsibility and the first class of four began their studies in October 1983. NEGST granted its first degree in 1986. In March 2011, NEGST obtained its university charter from the government of Kenya and is now known as African International University (AIU).

When I first entered, it was located on what had been a chicken farm, and we slept in a converted chicken coop. Today, it is transformed and its fields are filled with all modern buildings for students and staff. But extremely importantly, and what matters to me most is the caliber of faculty and staff at NEGST. To me the sustainability of an institution lies within its human resources. NEGST is intentional about "training Africans to train Africans." Most of its faculty and staff are made up of past graduates. The late Vice Chancellor, Dr. Douglas Carew, was among its first graduates. The current Dean of Academic Affairs, Dr. James Nkansah, is also a graduate of NEGST.

It is similar with our school. Those who maintain LICC and take it to the next level may not have shared those early struggles we had when we were trying to raise money to buy land and wondering when it would be safe enough in Liberia to start building. Yet, they will have faced and will continue to work through struggles as they maintain what we started. To maintain LICC, we know we need to develop competent people who will be faithful to the vision and to the Lord. We need people of character. We need people who understand our purpose and who accept that purpose and will, adapting to the future as necessary, move LICC towards that vision. Their experiences with LICC may not be the same ones we had. With the basics completed or well on the way, they can begin to concentrate on what is needed to keep LICC thriving and moving forward. Their challenge will be maintaining and growing the dream.

There are other things we will need as well. We will need to build a team that will be able to maintain the national and international relationships that are so important to the ongoing success of LICC and its students. I have enjoyed working on a national and international level to support LICC and I look forward to continuing that role. However, I also know that we need more leaders working to build relationships if we are going to be able to continue to expand.

## Create Endowments

On November 8, 2014, at its annual leadership meeting in Chicago, the ULICAF Board approved the launch of an endowment which will provide a secure base of resources for LICC's program and faculty development. The endowment will also partially alleviate the need for raising funds for core support, and reduce dependence on specific funding sources. Because an endowment provides a steady stream of income from permanently invested funds, endowment gifts keep growing and giving from one generation to the next. *Endowment gifts are the most lasting and powerful resources a donor can give.* Your gift of any amount will provide the "seed" and allow us to commence this ambitious dream. Our initial goal is to raise ***$100, 000*** (one hundred thousand dollars) for the endowment.

We need other types of endowments and reliable sources of income. We hope to purchase 100–200 acres of land and plant cash crops. Cash crops are rubber, cocoa, coffee, palms, etc. Ideally, we will be able to purchase land and plant rubber or palm trees that could generate income for the institution.

Having reliable, steady sources of funds is important to our future. Currently, we rely on many volunteers. Even if they are paid, we often rely on people who make personal sacrifices to work at LICC. That is, they accept less than market rates for their labors. We are glad we have these people. We would not have been able to get as far as we have without them. However, the next person who does the job may not be able to go without a salary. They may not have another source of income like a supportive spouse or savings. They may have a family to support. So financial sustainability is very important to us. We need to be able to stand on our own two feet. We know we will not always be able to count on the level of donations and grants we have received. We do not want LICC to end because of that. This challenge is one we will not solve tomorrow, but it is one that weighs on our leadership and drives us to make LICC as productive as possible.

## Strong Board of Governance

By charter, the Board of Trustees is the legal custodian of the College and assumes the all-important responsibility for the total program of the College. It has direct responsibility for selecting and supporting the LICC President, for long-range planning, for obtaining the necessary financial resources and facilities needed for the educational program of the College, for establishing faculty personnel policies, for deciding the broad aims of the College program, and for reviewing and establishing policies needed to maintain and develop such a program.

We need to maintain a strong board of governance, which is the Board of Trustees, to guide LICC as it carries out its mission. This includes ensuring that we adhere to our core values, and, most importantly, that we remain Christian in character. To accomplish this goal, the Board of Trustees must be comprised of godly men and women. The Board of Trustees plays an important role in overseeing the work that God has given Liberia International Christian College (LICC) to do and in stewarding the resources that God has provided LICC to accomplish that work. Strong faith and good governance are critical success factors in fulfilling the Board's role.

> *Have confidence in your leaders and submit to their authority, because they keep watch over you as those who must give an account. Do this so that their work will be a joy, not a burden, for that would be of no benefit to you.* Hebrews 13:17 (NIV)

The Board of Trustees delegates major responsibility to the administration, faculty, and student body to determine and administer the specific policies of all phases of the intellectual, cultural, social, and religious programs of the College. Yet, it still must provide oversight of activities and involve itself where necessary to maintain the intent and vision of LICC.

Let me add here that the LICC Board of Trustees is not the ultimate authority at LICC; the founders ULICA (United Liberia Inland Church

Associates) of Liberia and ULICAF based in America, jointly have the ultimate authority. The LICC Board of Trustees has oversight of LICC while ULICAF and ULIC, jointly, have oversight of the LICC Board of Trustees. This creates a balance of power. ULICAF and ULIC must exercise oversight and encourage progress to the long-term goals, yet, they must do so in a way that makes the best use of the energy of the LICC Board of Trustees who are actively engaged in executing the vision.

## Moving Forward with Building Projects

In 2015, we expect to start the final building required for our Three-Stranded Rope approach. We expect to continue the construction of the second and third floor of the agriculture building. We have also obtained the Board's approval to commence constructing the community health center as funds are made available.

The third priority project is the chapel. The chapel is important to us, not just for worship, but because it is a chance to reach out to the local Ganta community. It will have other purposes as well: for example, it will be used for graduation ceremonies, weddings, funerals, gatherings, and for conferences and various types of meetings.

We are now working with a firm in Indianapolis to help with a detailed design. We have given them input like how many seats we want in the sanctuary and different functions that we have in mind, like Sunday school for children and a place for the choir to practice. As with our other buildings, we expect to build this one out of bricks, because that is what we have available to us! If necessary, we can make our own as we have had to do often in the past. We learned of this architectural firm from a Liberian, a member of the ULICAF advisory board. We expect they will use their creativity to give us a design that we can review and make further comments back to them for revision. Once the basic design is complete, they will go on to prepare a detailed design that we can use to start building.

Once we have built our chapel, we will have completed the foundation of the institution. The Three-Stranded Rope approach will be complete. However, we will not stop building then, although we may slow down to concentrate on other needs like building an endowment. For the foreseeable future, our hope is that LICC will be building and growing. Even when the basic buildings are complete, there will be other needs like increased faculty housing to address. Longer term visions, like having student housing, may not be needed, or happen, in the foreseeable future. The city of Ganta is close to the university and it is cheaper to let the students rent. However, LICC will be teaching students long after I have completed my race; so sometime in the future LICC might build student housing.

## Become a University with Four-Year Degree Programs

From the beginning, our hope and plan was to offer four-year university degrees. However, we did not have the resources to approach the government for that accreditation when we started. So, we focused on providing three-year programs (the conventional 2 years for an Associate's degree, plus 1 year for remediation of gaps in high school learning) and are accredited by the government for that. In our next strategic plan, one of the goals is to take LICC to the university level.

In 2013 we submitted the documentation requesting full accreditation for a bachelor's program. This required another inspection which was completed. After addressing the concerns highlighted in the inspection report, we will be able to resubmit. In the short term, our expectation is that we will be able to offer more programs like agriculture and nursing. In the long term, this is all part of our strategic plan and the coming to fruition of the work of many of our staff and volunteers.

There will be changes to make in going from a college to a university. For example, we will need to increase the number of administrative and teaching staff. Some positions we have desired, but have been able to survive without since current faculty or visiting faculty could cover a needed course or two; as a four-year university we will need to fill these positions and offer more courses. For some of our existing programs, we will have to make sure they meet a university level of competency. A number of courses will need to be added and that will necessitate adding faculty even if we offer some of them on a rotating basis. When teaching faculty members are added, support staff must also be added.

There are many signs that we eventually will be able to attain this accreditation. In 2013, a President from a respected African University came to visit. The President wrote a nice letter saying that he was very impressed by what we were doing at LICC. We have gotten many accolades, but still this is an amazing thing to me. We started so small and really not that long ago. It is amazing what God has allowed us to accomplish in such a short time. Government personnel who have visited have been very positive and compared LICC favorably with other Liberian schools, most of which have been in existence much longer than LICC.

We were fortunate to invite the Minister of Education of Liberia and the County Director of Education to visit our campus. In a God moment, I learned they were visiting Ganta and invited them. They were very complimentary and said we compared well with the best of schools in Liberia. The accreditation standards are very rigorous and the Ministry of Education and the Higher Education Ministry have been shutting down schools that did not comply. So, we do have a big challenge before us, but with God's help, we are confident that we can meet it.

We look forward to being able to offer four-year bachelor's degrees. Even now our students are qualified to pastor existing churches or start new ones. However, the bachelor's degree, besides allowing us more time to teach our students and give them a better and more complete background, will allow our students more options and opportunities. Established churches that might not consider them with a two-year degree may hire them. A four-year degree would enable them to teach religious education in public schools. And they would be qualified and ready for more advanced degrees, like a master's or doctorate, should they desire. Eventually, we want and need some to come back to LICC to teach.

## Offer Professional Development and Other Forms of Ongoing Study

One day we also hope to offer Master's programs. We expect to start on that path by offering Master's level seminars so that the working professional can improve his or her skills. This will be another chance to serve our community. It will also give us another opportunity to become known in our community as an effective educational institution. Professionals who do not have the time for a full Master's program could still benefit from quality seminars. Hopefully, this involvement will help our full-time students, as it will provide us links to the local business community for employment or internships for students and graduates.

Another area we are looking at is vocational training. Perhaps we would house this training at our current campus, or open another site to focus on this training. Clearly not all careers require a four-year degree. Many of the skilled craftsmen that will be required to build and maintain Liberia fall in this category. Someday we envision being able to offer vocational training to become a mechanic, or an electrician, or a construction worker. Right now, many major projects in Liberians have large contingents of workers from Ghana or other countries because of a lack of skilled Liberians.

## Increase Student Numbers and Diversity

We will continue to strive to have a diverse student body. In our first class we had students from 7 of the 15 Liberian counties. While this was wonderful, our goal is that one day we will have students from all 15 counties. We would also like to have students from other countries (thus, the *International* in Liberian International Christian College). For example, Ganta is very close to Guinea (on the border with it) and Cote d' Ivoire (the Ivory Coast) is about 50 miles away. We would like to see more students from these countries be able to get a good education at LICC. Part of our dream is to see LICC be recognized throughout West Africa (particularly our neighboring countries) for offering a good education. We look forward to their taking what they have learned back to help their own countries.

To support this, we know we will have to put more focus on recruiting students and also on supporting them while they are at LICC. I know what it is like to go to school in a distant country. Even with the better communication tools we have today, like cell phones and the Internet, it is personally hard to be so far from friends and family. There are practical considerations as well. The student does not have friends or family to help if an emergency occurs or another need arises. If a family emergency requires the student's presence, getting back home can present much more of a challenge. In our future, I see a renewed emphasis on staff, like a Dean of Students, and a writing center and career planning center that will be taking care of our students. We want to provide good customer service to our students so that when they go back to their communities they will give LICC a good recommendation and send more students our way and they will desire to support LICC.

# Chapter 16: Our Greatest Challen

# to Date

In founding ULICAF and building LICC, we faced many challenges. As with starting any major endeavor, it sometimes seemed like we faced new ones daily. I could list many more, but I would like to detail three of our greatest challenges.

## Challenge 1: Inspiring Liberian Refugees

Even if refugees are very glad to be safe, the refugee experience is traumatic. Refugees have so many needs and the new culture is typically so different, that it is very easy to feel overwhelmed by the day-to-day events of life. We wanted to reach out to Liberians; the desire was there. As the leadership of ULICAF, we needed to articulate an inspiring vision, but we also needed to convince our average members that together we could do this. Often, the first steps were to get them to think outside of themselves and their immediate issues and then help them believe that with their participation we could make a difference.

Many of the refugees felt they did not have enough for themselves, that they were struggling just to survive. The reality might have been different, but they did not feel that way. To them, giving anything would have pushed them over the precarious line between struggling to get by and not surviving. That is an especially hard place to be if you have a family. Certainly these people did not have enough to share. They might even have felt they and their family needed handouts from others. They might have been looking for help from others, feeling desperate.

Once they began to believe they could support our project, they needed to come to understand that what they individually could not do, but we as a group could do, would be enough to make a difference—that it was not futile to try. We could have looked for an "out," for a miraculous answer, perhaps a "Bill Gates" to come and make our problems go away. Maybe if they had heard about our plans, they would have come to our rescue and given us the money to make our dreams reality.

We had to convince people that this was something we could do ourselves as Liberian refugees. More than that, this was something we *needed* to start ourselves. We developed an attitude of "We *can* do this; let's do this together!" versus looking for a magic answer to our desire.

We made it a clear expectation from the beginning that we were not looking for Americans to build a college for us; we should, and could, build it for ourselves. It is our dream and we must own it. We did not want to build something that was dependent on America or even any one individual or group. We did not want something that would fall apart if American support went away. We wanted something that was intimately built into the Liberian community and did not depend for its survival on outside help.

Part of this was getting individuals to understand that 'all of us' were much stronger than we were individually. Individually we could spare little, but that little, taken together would accomplish a lot. We said, "If everyone gives a little, if everyone gives just $20 a month, what we plan is possible." An individual family might not be able to do much with $20 a month, but if 200 people came together, they eventually would be able to raise enough money to make a difference. Our collective effort could make a difference. As we worked our plan, we reinforced that by periodically and consistently showing the results of that giving.

## Challenge 2: Coming Together as a Group

I've mentioned the joke about Liberians not being able to field a soccer team in one East coast city. This divisiveness applies to more than just Liberian soccer players—this is a human condition. We struggled with our need to be part of a group to accomplish a project for Liberia versus our desires to follow our own individual needs. We struggled to work together because we are not all alike. Some of us were poor and some were (relatively) rich. Some of us were adjusting to life in America; some of us were still struggling. Some of us were young, perhaps still in school; some of us were fairly far along in our careers. We had members from many, many different tribes, something that frequently was used to separate us into different factions in Liberia.

To accomplish a big project, we needed to stick together in spite of our differences. Part of accomplishing this was building a clear picture of the vision and holding it up above anything else. However, I personally believe *the key was our common faith*. We needed to make that the emphasis to unite us against all that could be used to pull us apart. We were all one in Christ. We were brothers regardless of what tribe we were from. We were not working as Mano or Kpellé or Bassa or Gio or Kru or Grebo or Krahn or Gola or Gbandi or Loma or Kissi or Vai or Bella or Mandingo or Fanti or any other tribe. Our faith made us brothers.

One of the scriptures that helped us early on was:

> *The Spirit of the Sovereign Lord is on me, because the Lord has anointed me to proclaim good news to the poor. He has sent me to bind up the brokenhearted, to proclaim freedom for the captives and release from darkness for the prisoners, to proclaim the year of the Lord's favor and the day of vengeance of our God, to comfort all who mourn, and provide for those who grieve in Zion— to bestow on them a crown of beauty instead of ashes, the oil of joy instead of mourning, and a garment of praise instead of a spirit of despair. They will be called oaks of righteousness, a planting of the Lord for the display of his splendor.* Isaiah 61:1-3 (NIV)

This scripture from Isaiah resonated with Liberians. We had experienced a horrific civil war. As a nation, we were rebuilding. As a community in America, we were striving to help those we had left behind. In our meetings, we focused on the Bible, on the teaching of Christ, on the things that brought us together and that matter most. At one powerful meeting in

Chicago, we even followed the example of Jesus, by humbling ourselves to wash each other's feet.

## Challenge 3: Learning to Lead Big Projects

The third challenge I would like to talk about had to do with me. I was leading an effort in which I had little experience. I did not know anything about running a non-profit organization. I began to look for practical ways to learn what I needed to know. One of the resources I found was Truth@work run by Perry Hines and Ray Hilbert.

I was able to meet with other leaders of non-profits, many of whom were facing the same problems we faced. We were able to share each other's struggles and learn from each other. At the meeting there would be a special speaker. For example, a speaker came to talk about fundraising. This helped us a lot, as we were able to learn from his expertise as well as each other as we processed the new learning and put it into practice in our own organizations.

Another source of knowledge for me was management books. I read many, many of these books, and would usually have two or three books on my desk to get new ideas. Often it would be late at night when I read and I would think about how the reading applied to whatever current problem I was working—like raising money, or attracting partners, or organizing some new project.

I am a different person than when I started the journey of creating LICC over a decade ago, and I am thankful for the experiences that changed me. However, that growth came with its share of pain and trials. Temporarily, I may have shirked from a challenge from time to time, but in the end I have faced the obstacles in my path. And I have fought the good fight. A leader must first be able to discipline himself and direct his own life. Being the President of LICC has driven me to ask God to help me learn ways to change for the better and I am grateful for that.

# Chapter 17: Leadership Continuity at LICC

I will not always be here to lead LICC, even if I never retire, I will eventually go the way of all men and go to that far better place—heaven. The work of LICC will not end with my death. So at some point, we will need a new leader for LICC. This applies, of course, to all our leadership positions at LICC. It is more immediately true for those positions currently filled with older and more experienced leaders. All organizations experience "turnover," as God's plan for individuals' lives leads them to new opportunities outside their current positions.

## Start with the Leaders

Because people are important to an organization and because some people will leave, most organizations have some type of succession planning process. Often times, the first focus is on leaders. Leaders are very important for organizations; the way the leadership goes is often the way the organization goes. If the leaders make good decisions, the organization goes well. If the leaders make poor decisions, the organization suffers. If the leader can communicate the vision, people follow; if the leader fails to communicate, the organization drifts. It is important to have financial resources, but without good leaders, finances will not matter and may be squandered or used ineffectively. An organization can have all the resources it would want, but it will not do any good if things fall apart because of poor decisions. Resources are important, but first an organization needs competent leaders.

If LICC fails to continue to develop into the future, I believe it will not be because of a lack of resources, but it would be because of a lack of good leadership. There is a great need for what we do; there are people who will support us. We need good leaders who will put these two parts together. So one of the things we are working on at LICC and ULICAF is developing a process for succession planning.

This is very important to me personally. I want our organization to go on without me. I want our organization to not only be able to survive without me, but also to continue to grow and prosper. Our vision is bigger than what I could dream; it is bigger than all of us. We must commit to supporting it. I view this as critically important to the health of the organization.

In 2013, we started a discussion on succession planning and how we will perform this in our organization. Take for example, my own position as Executive Director of ULICAF. Transitioning to a new leader can take time. It can be reassuring to the organization if a leader does not just step down, but steps aside, maintaining a continued commitment to the organization.

## Leaders' Qualifications

In the succession planning process, one of the key things is determining what you are looking for in a leader. So, we needed to look at the type of people we want to hire. We needed to decide what specific attributes we want to emphasize. When we asked the question of what characteristics we were looking for, a few came to mind immediately: someone that is strong in their relationship with Christ; someone who has the academic qualifications to run an institution or a department of it; someone who is visionary, by which we mean we want someone who has a long view, combined with the passion and energy to make it happen; and someone who understands and believes in our vision. Let me add some details. Our leaders must be:

- **Christ-Centered.** Perhaps this should go without saying, but it is the most important qualification we would look for. They need to be a born-again Christian. They need to be a believer. It is a key part of our job description as you might expect for a Christian college. We want to make sure our program is Biblically sound. We are not just seeking to impart knowledge, but more than that, we are striving to preserve and share the knowledge of the Bible. Values are critical. If your heart is not in the right place, then ten qualifications and vision will not matter.

- **Qualified.** Particularly as we are an educational institution, we look for leaders who have made a commitment to education. Some of our leadership jobs require a Bachelor's degree; some require a Master's degree. As a former student himself (or herself), he (or she) will be better able to understand the needs of our students if he (or she) has a Master's or Doctorate than if we hired someone with little or no formal education.

  We also evaluate the leader's skills against the skills needed for the job. For example, leaders such as the Dean of Students and those who work in the Admissions Office recruiting students need to show they can understand and empathize with students. These jobs requires communications skills and skills in interpersonal relationships; someone without them would be better suited to some other role.

- **Visionary.** A good leader will have a good grasp of the big picture and be able to articulate the big picture to others in a way that makes them want to join forces. He (or she) will be able to move forward with what resources are available. He (or she) will look for new resources and creative ways of solving problems. He must have enough confidence that having insufficient resources does not deter him from pursuing the goals of the organization. He should be able to tell of experiences in his past when he knew that if he was in God's will, the resources would come, even if patience must be exercised for a time. He must know that even when we are in God's will, it does not mean it will be easy. That is part of the visionary's life. He should buy into the vision as desirable and understand the reward is worth the work. When a leader believes in a vision, he will be sold out to it to the point that he will sleep with it and talk about it every chance he gets. This is important; our leaders must be sold on our vision before they can sell it to others.

I am sometimes asked how you can tell someone has vision. Though God knows the heart, we as humans are finite in our vision. We see the outward man and his actions first. We are fallible, but our hope is that God is in control and will help us with this, so prayer that God will lead us to people of vision is critical.

Actions will give a look into the heart of man. I can get a good idea of a leader's strengths by his or her approach to issues. When presented with a difficult task, how does the person respond—how has he dealt with difficult tasks in the past? Does he place the value of a project to the organization ahead of the difficulties that may arise? Is he generally hopefully, generally optimistic? Does he seem more concerned about God's call in his life than what others may think? If he talks about his dreams for himself, are those dreams reasonable but challenging? Does he suggest a realistic plan for achieving those dreams?

I would add another feature of this: inspiring teamwork. A leader must inspire, but a leader must also be able to bring people together to work as a team. We can help build this ability in our leaders, but is important that there are signs the individual understands this concept, so there is something we can build on. This can be difficult to address, because sometimes it is a matter of chemistry, or some might call it charisma. How do you tell if someone has that? Usually, his past experience and accomplishments will show he is able to build a team around an objective.

- **Vision Sharers.** It is very important that leaders share *our* vision. It is also important that they understand a vision seen only by a single leader is insufficient to generate a strong movement that can accomplish great things. Leaders must inspire others to see the exciting future. Then they must persuade the organization that it is achievable, that there are paths to get there. The leader must be able to communicate hopes and dreams so that his followers clearly understand and share them as their own. The leader must show others how their values and interests are served by the long-term vision of the future. When visions are effectively shared, they attract more people, sustain a higher level of motivation, and withstand more challenges. The leader must ensure that what he sees is communicated in a way that others can see it too. To do this, all of our leaders must see the reason for a full commitment, and challenge and inspire others to commit too.

Several years ago, we had the vision to make quality education "affordable and accessible to all Liberians, to improve their learning experience and empower them to share Christ across nations." We saw the lack of quality biblical education stopping the majority of young Liberians Christians from doing their very best and becoming fully-involved citizens of their nation. We believed that we would achieve our goals through Liberia International Christian College (LICC). None of us were focused on fame or fortune; it was all about "making a difference" for Christ.

Another element of shared vision is to constantly think up innovative ways to keep the vision flourishing. The leader's efforts must go beyond what he (or she) is currently occupied with today. It is true, the leader must encourage his team to work on what needs to be done today, but at the same time, the leader must also be thinking about what he and his team will be undertaking after their current work is complete. The leaders must constantly think "a few moves" ahead and picture future possibilities. This is a lot of work!

For example, as of this writing, ULICAF and LICC are focused on completion of the Community Resource Center. I am, too, but I am also thinking heavily about what is (or should be) next and making inquiries into the best way to accomplish it. A "Shared Vision" leader must be "compelled" in order to put in the time, suffer the inevitable setbacks, endure the criticism, and make the necessary sacrifices to forge ahead.

- **Aligned.** We want future leaders to buy into the vision God has given to us. As part of this, we had to make sure we were clear in our own vision. They should know, at the end of the day, that if we are to continue our success we must be aligned with God. This is not about doing it our way; we have taken our vision as far as we have because we stay aligned with God's work in Liberia. It should not be about doing things our way.

  Part of that shared vision is that we look for leaders who believe in our vision of development. We are not about relief. That is not our focus. There are plenty of good organizations working on various forms of relief in the world today, but that is not our purpose. We are developing people. We are discipling people. Our call is not just to put shoes on their feet. Our call is to show them how to make shoes for themselves and others and, in the process, how to put those shoes on and walk the path of Christ.

We will be looking for leaders that God wants to use to take our organization to the next level. We will be looking for leaders who will sustain what we have already built. One of the challenges our new leaders will face is how to maintain LICC. They will be inheriting something that is built, both figuratively and literally, but they still must refine it, and maintain it, and keep it clean so that it does not fall apart.

## God on the Succession Planning Team

We are starting with the assumption that ULICAF and LICC will need a new leader. Based on that assumption, our first step is to identify and prayerfully consider possible candidates. Our second step is to ask God to give us a new leader from these candidates. We need to come together in consensus on who that new leader should be. Our experience tells us we should not be looking for a specific person as much as we should be open to the person wanted by God. This means we need to approach these issues prayerfully. God often brings the unexpected. I think maybe this is because He is God, He is sovereign, and He delights in showing that His work in our lives is not restricted by what we can imagine or what we believe should be done. He can do more than we dream and, if we let him, He will.

Who (other than God) knows who that might be? We can guess, but it is better to go to God in prayer. Corporate or collective prayer is the place to start. We also need the prayers of many individuals, including you, the readers of this book. If it is important enough, individuals are called to pray and fast. This is the final challenge, trying to reach consensus as a group on God's choice for that position.

For example, it is possible that the best person for a position of leadership will not even be a Liberian. He or she might be a European or an Asian. We exist to educate Liberians and other West Africans, so this would surprise us some! However, our organization needs to be open to God's leading, even if His answer seems odd to us. Our next leader might be a woman. In this we might not be too surprised since the current President of Liberia is a woman.

## Adequate Transitional Period

If an organization is fortunate, it has time to transition to the new leader. There will be opportunities for the new leader to be mentored, learning from present leaders and getting acclimated. This would be ideal for us.

Sometimes the transition is more abrupt, and the organization has to scramble to find a replacement for a leader. In that case, of course, it is normal to appoint an interim leader who is familiar with the history and current situation while the search goes on for the leader's long-term replacement.

## Leader Candidate Success

In succession planning, another question to be answered is where you look to find your leaders. Some organizations are known for only (or primarily) promoting from within. This is hard for us at LICC, because we are still growing and do not have that many people to promote! When we do promote, it means that another position is then opening up, creating a need to back-fill for the person we just promoted—often meaning we have to recruit outside LICC for that position.

So, we are often looking to hire from outside LICC. When hiring from the outside, we look in several different areas for leaders. In particular, we do consider hiring our graduates. We look for people who are known to our Board or our current workers. In Liberia we advertise for some positions, particularly those that are hard to fill because they require credentials that not many people have.

We promote from within and hire externally as our needs require. However, our preference is to promote from within because we know the candidate is already part of our team and already understands the vision. Usually it takes less time for them to start contributing fully to LICC.

## Leadership Development

We also believe in the importance of developing our own leaders. So, we have sent staff and faculty to receive further education. For example, our Director of Finance went to Anderson University. Upon graduation, he returned and now serves as Vice President for Finance and is in charge of the business department where he will be teaching business classes. He is an example of ways we are growing people within our organization.

## Spousal Support

Our experience at ULICAF has shown that a leader needs the strong support of his or her spouse. Of the people I know personally, those who have their wife, or husband if a woman, behind them have an easier time. The energy and unity that come from having a common goal are strengthening. They are bound together in resolve. I think this is because the leader is putting much of his energy into the organization. That is an energy synergy that comes from the couple if the spouse is supportive of the organization and its goal, and they are in agreement as to the plan. The leader can move forward in spending time, energy, and money toward accomplishing the goal. God seems to bless those couples who work together faithfully; it is a spiritual thing. Even if time and money are tight, the spouse can understand the sacrifice they are making as a family to support the growth of the organization or initiative. I can attest to this fact as my wife constantly reminds me of our offerings every Sunday morning or as we visit other events that might need donations. I do not carry a checkbook with me all the time. So, we resolved the issue by giving Yah a checkbook to keep in her bag. And, believe me, only in a rare occasion will ladies forget their bag whenever they leave the house, and it is always good to turn to her and consult her, then be in agreement as we write a check for gifts.

Those whose spouses do not agree with their focus and passion find their commitment more difficult. Those leaders do not do well in giving of their time and energy, or most other organizational work. They constantly have to justify their actions to their spouse who sees the organization as taking away from the family—which often causes resentment or anger issues. Over the years, I have experienced that young ULICAF members who love and respect their spouses and work together as a team in marriage do much better in their roles within ULICAF than those who do not or who have troubled marriages.

## Succession Planning Applies to Other Positions

Leaders are important, but planning for change applies to other positions as well. What is a college without good teachers? The students do not come to LICC because I am President, but because of the quality of the teaching and the respect their education will receive in the community. As the President of LICC and the Executive Director of ULICAF, I wish all our good workers would stay with us forever. However, I know that will not be the case, so we need to continue to be open to all of those who express an interest in working with us.

In our recent ULICAF Board annual meeting in Chicago, the Board boldly adopted an LICC decision making matrix. The Board was careful to put in place a governing commission made of five representatives, three from ULICAF and two from our primary church partner in Liberia. The matrix is also specific about the roles of the members of the LICC Board of Trustees, the President and all stakeholders. This is very important as we move forward. It allows the school to grow and to continue to be guided by godly men and women in fulfilling its vision of faithfully training and equipping Christian leaders for the nation and the Church.

# Chapter 18: My Next Journey

## Point of Decision

In August of 2013, I had the opportunity to attend the Global Leadership Summit at Grace Church, Noblesville, Indiana. General Colin Powell (former U.S. Secretary of State) was among the speakers and was terrific. I purchased his latest book, *It Worked for Me: In Life and Leadership*, for details on his talk. In the seventh chapter, I was struck by a unique heading: *"Where on the Battlefield?"*

The General shared his experience about an insightful letter he had received from an older United States Ambassador Kennan. In the letter, Ambassador Kennan reminded the new Secretary of State of the Founding Father's intention around the two principal functions of the Secretary of State. First, the Secretary must function as the "President's most intimate and authoritative advisor on all aspects of American foreign policy." Second, the Secretary was to "exercise administrative control over the State Department and the Foreign Service." The letter then concludes, "You cannot properly perform either of these duties if you are constantly running around the world in your airplane."

On reflection, General Powell realized that Ambassador Kennan's letter was actually about finding the right balance in life. Where should the commander (strategic leader) of an organization be on the battlefield? The answer is: "where he can exercise the greatest influence and be close to the 'Point of Decision'." The location of the "Point of Decision," as Colin explains, is a function of a leader's experience, self-confidence, confidence in his people, and the needs of his superior. For me, the leader's "Point of Decision" is the place where I can best see what is really going on, best influence the outcome, and yet also still be available to God (my superior) for His direction. The prophet Micah said,

*He has showed you, O mortal [man], what is good. And what does the Lord require of you? To act justly and to love mercy and to walk humbly with your God.* Micah 6:8 (NIV)

For ULICAF and LICC, three of my goals at the "Point of Decision" are to (1) provide the strategic leadership LICC needs to grow into a reputable Christian University, (2) remain committed to networking with my friends and partners (existing and new) to develop the necessary financial resources needed to finish building LICC, and (3) my final goal is to develop the leadership (new and existing) who will sustain LICC far into the future.

What is next for me? Now that LICC is up and running, I do not intend to rest on my laurels. I like the words of the Apostle Paul:

*Not that I have already obtained all this, or have already been made perfect, but I press on to take hold of that for which Christ Jesus took hold of me. Brothers, I do not consider myself yet to have taken hold of it. But one thing I do: Forgetting what is behind and straining toward what is ahead, I press on toward the goal to win the prize for which God has called me heavenward in Christ Jesus.* Philippians 3:12–14 (NIV)

I do know (or at least believe in faith) that I will always be involved in some way with LICC. Practically, there are things like fundraising that will likely benefit from my involvement for the foreseeable future. I have worked hard in this area and only a few within ULICAF have the story I have and the abilities and passion to tell our story well. Even when I am able to lay down the other duties of LICC, I may still need to be involved in this role. I do not mind. I look forward to continuing to tell people about LICC and share my passion for education, and educating my countrymen.

What is God telling me about my future? I'm not completely sure. I do not hear loud prophetic voices, but only the still, quiet voice and that only occasionally. For much of God's plan, just like most Christians, I have to wait for time and circumstance to provide some direction. Often, it is the closed doors that have directed me to a path left open, a path that has taken me closer to the fruition of God's plan for my life. I do know this from my study of God and His Word: God will take what we give Him and use it to His glory. I believe, in faith, He wants to expand our work in Liberia. For God to do so, it will take full commitment and trust in Him. If we continue with that level of commitment and trust, He will continue to bless us.

## Mentoring

In finishing the race well, one of the things I would like to do more of is mentoring. I think of an old person's prayer:

> *Even though I am old and gray, do not leave me, God. I will tell the children about your power; I will tell those who live after me about your might.* Psalm 71:18 (NCV)

I am committed to live for the next generation. The wisdom is that when you live only for your own generation, your vision will perish. We need to concern ourselves with those leaders who will follow us. I do not have to look far. Some of the best leaders to be trained are among my graduating students of LICC. I have already hired eight out of the 100 students that have graduated. In the future, I look forward to hiring more of our graduates. They will help us take the college that trained them to the next level—like African International University or Hope College. I would envision some of our students pursuing further studies, returning to Liberia, and serving the college in various positions—even as the President or Vice President of Academic Affairs, or Dean of Students.

I would like to spend more time coaching and inspiring the next generation. I would like to spend more time helping young students. I want to help them go further than I have. I want to help them build a Liberia in their lifetime that is even greater than the one I believe I will see during my life on this earth.

And this is possible. God used a man of God to bring me to Him. Then, God changed my life and taught me how to share with others, so that I would share my faith, and some would come to believe. Then, He changed, and continues to change, their lives, too.

## Sustainability

So, even though my love for LICC is unabated, I also am working to make LICC sustainable even when I am less involved. For regardless of other plans, I will not live forever and LICC will go on after my time has passed. This is the reason that LICC, like other organizations, does succession planning. LICC is more than any one person; it is the sum of all our work for many years and the many sacrifices that we made to make this dream a reality. So I continue to prepare people for service in God's work. And my hope is that they prepare the generation after themselves, so that they too will become disciples of Christ and pass on to the next generation what is entrusted to them—our faith and also the vision that is LICC.

God called me to do this work; He prepared me to do this work in ways I did not understand at the time. I think of all my schooling! I loved school, but it seemed never-ending at times. Without it, I could never have helped to shape this dream or lead LICC through its beginning and heavy growth stage. Only God knew what I would need. Yet, I am also helping Him prepare others so that they will carry on our dream. So, at some point, there will be a time—or several times—of transition as I let go of some of my duties at LICC.

## Open to God's Leading

For my part, I need to think about what is next. The vision of LICC has been so much a part of me for so long that is hard to imagine anything else. So I continue to serve God at LICC, but I also remain open to His leading. It is hard to know how or where God will lead next, but I know I need to be open to opportunities.

Now is not a time for retirement, but soon may be a time to rise to the next challenge. Whatever God calls me to, I will work to do it well for His glory and so finish well the race before me.

It is not good to place restrictions on God. For one thing, sometimes it seems like He delights in assigning us to duties we say we loathe (that He might show us He works even there). However, and I say this to my reader and myself, we should let go of preconceived notions of what God wants us to do. This is a matter of trust. There is nothing but that we should trust God. He will never lead us astray. He will lead us only to what is right. He will not call us to do anything that cannot work out for good in the long run. My Christian friends, you know the verse as well as I do:

> *And we know that in all things God works for the good of those who love him, who have been called according to his purpose.* Romans 8:28 (NIV)

So, again, I say this to myself as well as my readers: do not put restrictions on what God wants to do with your life. Work to have a conviction that you will do what God wants you to do. God rarely calls us to a labor we truly hate; yet He will often call us to a labor we find difficult and that makes us uncomfortable, or that we think is beneath us.

**I am a life-long learner.** I have been in school most of my youth and adult life. And, even though I may no longer be a registered student at a particular school, I want to continue learning. I like reading good books and, hopefully, I can write some more books. Bill Hybels, founder of Willow Creek Church and the Global Leadership Summit, advises leaders to read all they can. There is also the scripture to read and re-read. I am to "lead diligently." How does one lead diligently when there is so much to read and learn? I want to constantly get better at leading people at our institution, and the only way to do that is to become a voracious reader. When you read, you collect classic and new information and add to your thoughts. A few years ago, I read Bill Hybels' book called *Axiom*. From reading the book I discovered Bill's advice to a leader on what to look for when trying to hire a staff on your team included his 3 C's of Character, Competence and Chemistry which I referred to earlier as having become keys in how we choose new staff.

In his book *Half Time: Changing Your Game Plan from Success to Significance*, Bob Buford explained the importance of second half learning (the second half of your life). In my first half, learning was focused on career and success. In my second half, my learning is becoming focused on "unlearning the doctrine of specialization." My second half learning will move me toward a more holistic approach to leadership and to the world. It will also demand more of me. When the mind is empty, there can be many distractions. So, I will continue to concentrate on learning good and wholesome things in order to protect my mind from the debasing things that are easily absorbed.

What to learn is another important question for me. First, I believe continuing to study the Bible is extremely important. The Bible was written by 40 human authors under the supernatural inspiration of God, and is our authority for all matters of faith and practice. I have been reading and studying the Bible for years. I have read the entire Bible several times. Even so, I continue to learn new things from it.

Second, I want to learn anything that will help me accomplish this mission God has called me to. As I write this chapter, I have registered with Overseas Council in Indianapolis to participate in a pilot program for newly appointed seminary presidents called FLITE (Foundation for Leadership in Theological Education). The aim of this program is to help new presidents develop a high level of competency in seminary leadership. The program is a 12-month commitment which includes a five-day workshop and online reading and mentoring. FLITE will have a particular focus on five core practices of seminary presidents identified in a study conducted by the Auburn Center for the Study of Theological Education. These core practices are: Team Building, Faculty Relationships, Financial Management, Institutional Advancement, and Vision.

Because I am heading and developing a newly-established academic institution, I will make use of conferences, workshops, seminars, and study in the areas of business, technology, management, leadership, and related subjects.

**I am a pastor.** I have been performing some type of work in the church almost since I became a Christian. So, if an opportunity in business presented itself, should I ignore it out of hand? At one time in my life, my answer would have been "yes": yes, I should ignore what I would have felt was a "temptation." I was working and studying to become a better pastor, not a businessman. Today, I see it differently. I would pray and then ask for God to give me discernment.

Let me be more specific. I would ask for discernment between what is right and what is almost right. What the world knows as the best choice may be what is almost right in the sight of God and, therefore, is to be refused (so we can do what is right and best in God's eyes). For me, being able to make more money, or even much more money, would not be the deciding issue. However, impacting people's lives is not exclusive to pastors. A businessman can impact the lives of many people also. The decision would not be about money, but about following God's plan for my life. The deciding issue would be whether this is what God wants me doing next.

**I am a teacher.** I have taught at many different levels in my life from grade school to college. I am a Christian teacher; I believe in sharing God's word. During my term at LICC, I plan to teach two courses during an academic period. I will offer to teach personal evangelism and discipleship and also introduction to philosophy. My love of soul-winning and discipleship stems from personal experience. It was Dr. Amos Miamen (current President of ABC University) who, for the very first time, clearly introduced me to the possibility of eternal life. That introduction created the spark that lit that flame of a revolution that swept the Holy Spirit into my life and gave me new life. Dr. Miamen's work did not stop with this introduction, but was followed by several years of mentoring. It is amazing that even to this date, he has never stopped calling to check on me and to find out how Yah and the children are doing. He reminds me constantly how his own faith is still growing or how his faith has come under attack, but how God by His grace, has delivered him and given him peace.

I love philosophy because it stimulates our thoughts and thinking. I want to engage our young and high-potential students coming to LICC to think beyond food hunting and gathering (beyond merely obtaining education for careers). I believe in every Christian's heart a spark is glowing. If fed and nurtured it will become a glowing fire for Christ. I want to be able to light fires in these young men and women. That is the energy I see in the eyes of young Liberian students, and my prayer is that they will have the courage to live the dreams that God has placed within them.

I am reminded of Jesus and Simon's story described by the Apostle Luke. Prior to the encounter, Simon has been engaged in a small family fishing business venture, and loyal to that tradition. But then Jesus approached him, and asked Simon to cast his net into the deep water. Despite Simon's past experience evidenced by the night-long struggle for a catch, he immediately obeyed Jesus' command and let the net down into the deep water. Instantaneously, his new faith was rewarded with a "great catch"— so great that he had to seek help to secure the fish onboard. And the new experience transformed Simon into a "fisher of men instead of fish" (Luke 5:1). The lesson: In many ways, we are like Simon with past experience which is sometimes the barrier that stops us from moving forward. But where we let go of our experience and let faith take its place, we too can be rewarded and transformed to do greater things.

Does all this mean I should only work for a Christian college or school? Again, you know the answer to this as well as I do. If I worked in the Education Ministry for the Government of Liberia or for one of its counties, I would have the opportunity to impact many more students that I can today at LICC. Working for the government would place me in a position where I would have to deal more regularly with politics and be more publicly known. While I am the face of LICC to the outside world, I do not think of this as one of my strengths. My current political

216

involvement is listening to the news and trying to understand where my country is going next. However, I need to remain open to where God may lead. You do too.

Becoming the principal of a grade school or high school could be in my future. Someone might say, "but Sei, you are head of a college, even if it is a new and small one, how could you go back to overseeing grade schools?" It might seem like a step back to them, but I do not see it the same way. We need to pray and seek the mind of the Lord. God is trying to bring good to Liberia. God is trying to help Liberians live in peace and recover economically. God is working in Liberia through more than just LICC. Neither do I feel like it is beneath my dignity to go from being a big fish in a small pond to a small fish in a large pond. LICC is not the only college in Liberia; many colleges are springing up and older ones are growing. I need to be open to going where God leads even if it is to a place I had not thought God would find a way to use me.

**I am a Liberian.** I grew up in Liberia and I have spent most my adult life working to help Liberia or other countries in West Africa. It makes human sense that God would use me that way. These are my people. Even so, should I put a restriction on God, saying, "Let me serve you anyway you think best, Lord, but only if it is in Liberia"? I think the right (and even best) answer is obvious to both of us. I am committed to my countrymen, but I have travelled widely since my youth and I will tell you something we all know deeply in our hearts, even though from time to time we ignore it. All people are the same in at least this: They have a deep and abiding need for God. I know that many ignore this. For that matter, I know that many ignore this for their whole lives, no matter how much the Holy Spirit convicts or how much their Christian friends and relatives share with them. Knowing that the fields are ripe for harvest all over the world, should I place a restriction on God's path for me? Again, we know the answer to this as Christians. Even though it might lead to an uncomfortable path, I need to be open to going anywhere in the world that God might call me to minister.

This is somewhat hard for me. The reason is simple. Though it was often confusing on the journey, looking back I can see how God worked in my life to bring me to the place I am today as founding President of LICC. God has called me in this time (the end of the 20th century and beginning of the 21st century) and place (United States and Liberia) and He gave me the resources I would need to fulfill that role. From my youngest days, He grew me in specific ways. It is true I had a passion for learning (God given); it is true I worked and studied very hard; however, it is also true He gave me many opportunities to study and improve my education. He directed my path and provided a way when, sick of school, I went on to get a PhD at Loyola.

There are good biblical examples of God calling people to a specific people and context as well. Moses? He was called to lead the Jews out of Egypt, not lead or help lead the Egyptian nation as might have been the case with his upbringing in Pharoah's household. (Exodus chapter 3) The Apostle Paul? He was called to be the Apostle to the Gentiles and not the Jews.

My first duty is not even to Liberia. My first duty is to God and the universal church of all believers. If I want God's presence to go with me night and day, then I need to be walking the path God has laid before me. If God's plan for me includes working in ministry in some place in the world other than Liberia, then I need to be open to that leading. It is true I am more comfortable living and working in Liberia and United States. It is true I seem to have been preparing all my life for this role as founding President of LICC. It is also true that many of the skills I have developed and many of my experiences can be transferred to other locations, situations, and peoples. God is a god of miracles, and of mystery, and of great, and often, difficult love. I will stay in Liberia if that is what He wants me to do, but I will go elsewhere if that will help God advance His kingdom.

# Chapter 19: The Outbreak of Ebola Virus in West Africa

## Liberia Ebola Virus Crisis: Setbacks and New Opportunities

This chapter is written out of necessity. It was not part of the original plan. We had planned to submit the manuscript to reviewers and have it ready for publication in October, 2014. However, an event of serious magnitude, the Ebola Virus outbreak, caused the writing of this chapter. So, my editor asked me to add this chapter and shed some light on our national crisis and the shutting down of all public and private institutions.

On June 21, 2014, my wife and I were fortunate to visit LICC for our 3rd graduation and the dedication of our Community Research Center (library and technology center). We were joined by 21 excited international friends and supporters. It was a time of joy. It was also a time for us to reflect on the path we had taken to launch LICC and to remember how much God has led us on our journey. The plans immediately after the graduation were to begin the electrification of the college campus and complete the construction of our agriculture building (a three story building).

Yah and I were beginning to be convinced that the time was ripe for our return after more than 20 years outside of Liberia. After the graduation, we would return to the States, sell our Indiana home, return to Liberia, and live on campus to continue the development of the college.

Then on July 6, the commencement speaker in her speech alerted us to a national crisis that was brewing. Three months prior to the graduation event, a deadly virus called "Ebola" had viciously attacked the neighboring Guinea. The speaker cautioned that the virus had entered Liberia through the northern border between Sierra Leone and Liberia, and Nimba was one of the at-risk counties.

Barely a week after the graduation, the forecast of the commencement speaker became a full-blown virus outbreak—an epidemic. The **deadly Ebola virus** which first started in the nation of Guinea, spread into Liberia and the city of Ganta where the LICC campus is located.

Liberia would eventually have a higher death rate than its neighbors Sierra Leone, Guinea, and Nigeria. The Ebola virus, like HIV, is spread through human social behavior. Ebola is spread by unsanitary burial practices when burying someone who has died of Ebola and by contact with the bodily fluids (blood and saliva) of an infected person. It is said to have an incubation period of 2–21 days and progresses uncontrollably. Until this writing, there has been no report of any proven vaccine or cure for the disease. Two American doctors and a nurse have survived after being flown out of Liberia to an infectious-disease-controlled hospital in Atlanta, Georgia. All three victims survived when they were treated with experimental drugs.

## The Immediate Impact

The government of Liberia established a 90-Day State of Emergency to help contain the virus. That mandate shut down all public and private institutions, restricted movements of people, and closed all borders. This mandate has turned a weak economy into a disastrous economy.

*On August 8, Yah and I returned to the United States. We convened an emergency meeting with our Board to find solution. We quickly wrote to our friends and supporters and broke the sad story about the forced shut-down of LICC.* The letter said in part:

> "We are deeply saddened by the impact this has had on Liberia and on LICC. We have taken extra precautions by having all LICC staff work from home during this current period. Guarding the health and safety of our human resources is our top priority. We ask that you join us in prayer for Liberia and all of West Africa as they deal with this world health crisis and now economic crisis."

With the approval of ULICAF board, we committed to raise $45,000 to support the 37 employees at LICC and their 200 family members through this shut down period. While LICC was not open there was no income and the staff and their families risked insecurity in health care, lack of food, and threats to their physical safety.

## More Ebola Outbreak Impacts

Several more forecasts from the international media and health experts continued to seep into the country from different parts of the world. One forecast said that this outbreak of the Ebola virus is by far the largest in the nearly 40-year history of the deadly disease. As of the 13th of September, 2014, there were 4,269 cases and 2,288 deaths had been reported in the outbreak of the disease in Guinea, Liberia, Sierra Leone, and Nigeria according to the report from the World Health Organization (WHO). Conventional Ebola control interventions were not having an adequate impact in Liberia due to lack of medical care, low levels of education and thus understanding of good hygiene, family dedication, and a lack of understanding of the virus by the common person. However, intervention treatments were beginning to work elsewhere to limit the transmission—most notably in Nigeria, Senegal, and the Democratic Republic of Congo.

Another forecast from a UN special representative in Liberia warned that the Ebola crisis had become complex, with political, security, economic and social implications that will continue to affect Liberia well beyond the current medical emergency. He also said Liberians are now facing the gravest threat since the war—one that would challenge any government or society.

These forecasts forced President Ellen Johnson-Sirleaf to write a letter and implore President Obama for help in managing Liberia's rapidly expanding Ebola crisis. She also warned that without American assistance the disease could send Liberia into a deeper civil chaos than enveloped the country for two decades. Here is a clip I obtained from our President's letter to President Obama:

> *I am being honest with you when I say that at this rate, we will never break the transmission chain and the virus will overwhelm us. And, urgently [I am requesting] 1,500 additional beds in new hospitals across the country and [urging] that the United States*

*military set up and run a 100-bed Ebola hospital in the besieged capital, Monrovia.*

## Human Resource Impact

Liberia has been hit the hardest among all the infected countries—Guinea, Sierra Leone, Nigeria, and Senegal. The virus outbreak first started in Guinea, then spread across its borders into Liberia, Sierra Leone, Senegal and Nigeria. There are many fingers being pointed because of this, and the first finger points at the government of Liberia. When the virus was confirmed in Guinea, there was an immediate need to close the borders between Liberia and Guinea. But this did not happen. Because of the downplay of this virus outbreak, hundreds of lives were lost, mainly because the healthcare workers were unaware and unprotected. Secondly, due to the slow action of the government, ordinary Liberians engaged in total denial of the existing of the deadly disease. Both people and the government finally came to accept the fact after so many people had been infected and many had died. Very sadly, the already under-resourced healthcare workers in Liberia were particularly hard hit.

The United Liberia Inland Church, our primary ministry partner in Liberia, sadly lost a young nurse. Mercy Dahn graduated a few years ago, and took a position in Lofa County, the northern border between Liberia and Sierra Leone. She was unprotected, got infected, and died shortly afterwards. Mercy was the only daughter of her parents, Elder Thomas Dahn and his wife Ruth from Karnwee Inland Church.

At LICC, we lost a dear young friend. He was not a full-time employee, but came frequently to ask for day work so he could support himself while he was in school. He was infected along with his grandmother and his young brother. Unfortunately, all three died from the Ebola virus.

## Economic Impact

It's too early to know how large the economic impact of Ebola will be on West Africa and Liberia. Past experience, including the 2002-03 Severe Acute Respiratory Syndrome (SARS) epidemic in Asia, suggest it could be very large, especially in the African countries that have been hardest hit. Fortunately, actions that the U.S. and other donor countries took helped to not only control the epidemic, but also to minimize the economic fallout.

"Ebola is much more like Avian Flu and SARS than AIDS," Mead Over, Senior Fellow, Center for Global Development at the UN said, "Its gestation period is very rapid, and that stirs a panic that creates an economic impact." For example, he estimates the economic impact of SARS due to reduced trade, tourism, and investment was estimated at about $40 billion—the equivalent of $50 million per death. Because of the larger number of cases, Ebola could be worse.

Mead Over emphasizes, however, that the Ebola epidemic so far is tiny compared to the toll of malaria, tuberculosis, and HIV, "all of which are many multiples more deadly on a continuing basis."

## Containment and Recovery

In the case of Asia, the number of cases of SARS increased every week for two months before beginning to decline. The number of cases of Ebola continued to increase each week for many weeks, but, with the dramatic increase in national and international attention to the disease, the number of weekly cases eventually peaked and began to decline.

There is hope since the disease was contained relatively quickly. If the disease had not contained soon enough, fears would linger on year after year, and the impact would extend for much longer.

One serious economic impact in the affected areas is full air service. During the worst of the crisis, almost all airlines cancelled their flights to

Monrovia, Freedom, and Conakry. Thankfully, flights eventually resumed, but for a while Liberia was very isolated from the outside world.

With strong support of the people of the affected West African countries, the international fear of Ebola and the consequent aversion behavior towards these countries can be limited and the duration and magnitude of the economic consequences reduced.

Dr. Clement

Liberia was very fortunate to have leaders who responded to the crisis so proactively. Our President, Ellen Sirleaf was one of them. Another leader was Dr. Peter Clement.

Dr. Clement worked with local communities in Lofa County and Médecins sans Frontières (MSF). UN Security advised against travelling to Lofa. Fortunately, Dr. Clement decided to go anyway, travelling from Monrovia for 12 hours over dirt roads to Lofa, near the Guinea border.

The villages he would help had a history of hostility to each other. The Ebola crisis was leading people to fear each other again. Old hatreds were coming to the surface. Dr. Clement emphasized that Ebola was *the mutual enemy*—not each other.

Dr. Clement started by listening first. He patiently listened to the community to understand their fears, then he started to explain about the virus and how people can prevent from getting infected.

Once they knew what Ebola was and how to stop it, they declared together: "No more Ebola in our community from today."

### A Plan Developed by the Community

Immediately, the people living in the community came up with their own plan and made sure that it spread to all the households. They said:

- Ebola is a disease, not a curse, not a government plot.
- Those that are sick must go to the MSF clinic in Foya.
- No one can bury their loved ones anymore. Effective immediately they would call the people who do it safely.
- Although they are a very friendly people, there would be no more physical contact when greeting one another.

Dr. Clement carried the same approach around the county, community by community.

The impact was significant. Soon there were only a few patients in the MSF clinic in Lofa and it was the first place in the country where an Ebola clinic downsized their number of beds (from 140 to 40).

### After the Outbreak

As of this writing, the Ebola crisis is basically over in Liberia. We are not celebrating complete victory over Ebola yet. What we can say is that only a few sporadic cases are emerging. Ebola is recognized for what it is. When these cases do emerge, we now have the strong resources to identify and address them. This includes treatment centers built with the help of the

International community. These centers are well-equipment and staffed with personnel who are experienced in recognizing and treating Ebola.

The government has also taken precautions to ensure schools are equipped to identify and respond to potential Ebola cases. If a case is suspected, the school personnel know to take suspected cases to a nearby treatment center.

In response to the crisis, LICC raised additional funding to hire new employees and setup security posts on campus. We also have an onsite nurse. This allows us to educate and enforce guidelines like making sure students wash their hands. One precaution we now take is to check student temperatures to ensure they don't have a fever. All of this is done to ensure the health and safety of our students, staff, and visitors.

We have made it through this crisis. LICC is open and educating students. LICC is once again inviting visitors to our campus.

# Chapter 20: We Invite You

## My Personal Invitation to You

I make my personal invitation to you: Consider visiting LICC as so many others of our supporters have done. We look forward to meeting you. For our Christian friends, we look forward to sharing the fellowship that is common to all believers.

## What You Will See If You Visit LICC

First, you will meet Liberians. Andrew Taylor, a British research fellow in Michigan, and I shared a room during my trip to Israel several years ago. Each night, we had conversations of all sorts before going to bed. One night, I invited Andrew to visit LICC and perhaps teach a course. His quick question was, "Sei, if I come to Liberia, what will I see?" I immediately supplied the answer, "Andrew, you will see 'People.'" What I actually meant was that when you come to Liberia you will meet some of the friendliest people on earth. I know this sounds like I am blowing my own trumpet (or at least Liberia's). However, Liberians are even more unabashedly friendly to strangers than their own fellow Liberians! In the 1990s, an Anglican Bishop in Uganda took me into his home and refused to allow anyone to accommodate me but himself. He behaved that way because when President Idi Amin was killing Ugandans, the bishop had escaped to Liberia where he had been treated wonderfully, so he wanted to personally return the favor.

Hopefully you will find, like most visitors do, that Liberians are a friendly and social people. Although there are 16 distinct tribes, you will probably not be aware of that and will see us all simply as Liberians.

When we started at LICC, you would have seen a stretch of barren ground with some forest if you had visited. That is what you would have seen with your eyes. What you would have seen when you looked with more than just your eyes, would have been hope—hope for a better life for our children and their children's children.

Now if you come to visit, you will see a functioning college or university. We have classrooms with students, a library and technology center, and an agricultural program. When you come, you will see a college that is reaching out to Liberians in the local community. You will be surprised to see a well-designed campus layout beautifully crafted and landscaped. We have introduced a tradition of excellence marked by the planting of beautiful trees from all over America, Africa, and from other parts of the world. You will see fruit trees and, in season, enjoy some of those fruits with us at our dinner table.

You will also see a college in progress. In fact, do not be surprised to see piles of bricks waiting to be used in some new construction project!

The most important thing you will see is students who are trying to build a better future for themselves and their community. The students will be males and females from all age groups and walks of life. They will be there to study and to meet people and prepare for future jobs and careers. And they will welcome you and want to get to know you.

## A Snapshot of Liberia

If you come to visit, you will see more than LICC. You will have the chance to see Liberia.

Our dry season is from October into February. The split between dry and wet seasons is about 50/50. We have about six months of dry weather and about six months of rainy weather. The dry season is when we do most of our construction work. We plant during the rainy season. This is partly because rain is very important to growing rice. In April we get some rain, but not too heavy, so we can plant corn and other vegetables. The heavy rains typically begin in July and go through September. Therefore, we plant rice in early May. In September there is very heavy rain and we wait for the crops to grow. From the end of October into November, is our harvest time. Besides rice, we like to eat meat and fish. Wild animal meat, when available, is a particular delicacy.

When you come to Liberia, you will see a land of hope and optimism. You will also see a Liberia that is still recovering from the civil war. The main focus of the average Liberian is the personal struggle to put food on the table and keep a roof over their family's heads. After that, they are focused on various things going on in Liberia, as well as hoping for continued development in their country.

The need for continued development is real. For example, with a population of 4.5 million people, we have only 150 doctors. So increasing the number of Liberian healthcare workers is a big focus. Although many modern roads are being built, many of the roads are still primitive; it can take quite a while to go from one place to another. So there is a lot of focus on building roads, bridges, and other infrastructure.

Investment is pouring into Liberia, and more investments are needed. Now that the rule of law is prevalent again, outside businesses feel it is safe to invest. Over 16 billion dollars has been put into Liberia and more is expected to follow. Service investments are of critical importance.

Little outside news gets to the average Liberian. This lack of knowledge about the outside world is partially because of the lack of current technology. There are few TVs in Liberia. For example in Monrovia, our most developed city, about 5% of the population have TVs. Even Internet access is restricted as it costs $50 a month for unlimited access. Compared to the United States or Canada, there are few news sources.

Cell phones are very popular with those who can afford them. It is relatively cheap to call from Liberia to America—it is more expensive to call Liberia from America. Radios, FM, and short-wave are relatively common, so some news and information gets distributed that way.

Along with several other African countries, Liberia has a low per capita Gross Domestic Product. Often it is less than $1,000 a year. With continued development and recovery from the civil war, that is expected to change. Even without GDP increasing, the safety that peace has brought has measurably improved the lives of all Liberians.

In our Liberian churches you will find passionate people who love Christ and work to share their faith with their community. Although my viewpoint is skewed somewhat by having attended mostly large churches while in America, I should mention that most Liberian churches are small. It is difficult to get enough money to build large ones. However, like in America, they are affiliated with each other through denominations.

## What Past Visitors Have Said

Let me tell you the reactions of some of our partners who have visited us. I have told you about my Wednesday evening strategic planning partner Russ. He supported us in various ways for many years before he made the trip to Liberia. Here is what he said about his visit to LICC:

> *Sei, my experience in Liberia deeply touched me. I have never felt more welcomed, more known, more loved, or more belonging than I did while I was there. The people I had been serving from a distance became "real" to me, and each story I heard was compelling. Proverbs 3:27 (NIV) says, "Do not withhold good from those to whom it is due, when it is in your power to act." How could I not serve tirelessly and with joy after personally seeing the good that was accomplished from my efforts?*

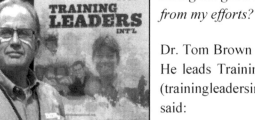

Dr. Tom Brown was a visiting professor. He leads Training Leaders International (trainingleadersinternational.org). He said:

*In 2014, I was thrilled to have the opportunity to return [to Liberia] and to be connected to ULICAF. I wondered what effects of the civil war I would encounter. It was so encouraging to find a spirit of hope and love of country among those I met.*

*I met a young lady named Caroline who is pursuing a nursing degree and intends to practice in Liberia. She seems to not be looking for a way out of Liberia, but [a way] to serve the future of Liberia. That is why I want to help her with her education and dreams.*

*My time with the students was fantastic and the most valuable experience was knowing and feeling the hearts of my students. The students were so engaged in the class and I am anxious to hear their feedback on the class.*

*I had the privilege of spending time with Dr. Buor as he told of his hope for Ganta and Liberia. I imagine that many come to Africa from America to experience the wonders of Africa. I believe those wonders are found in the hearts of Liberians. I got a taste of that on this visit and I want more.*

The Lord willing, Dr. Tom Brown will return to LICC for four weeks to teach another pastoral course in 2016.

Pastors Dave Rodriguez and Keith Carlson with LICC Students

In 2011, we invited Pastors Dave Rodriguez and Keith Carlson from Grace Church to visit LICC. The primary purpose of the trip was to investigate the feasibility of ULICAF/LICC entering into a strategic partnership with Grace. Ruth Schwartz, our Treasurer, came to provide financial consulting and Russ Schwartz came to provide computer consulting. All four planned to teach short courses while on campus. While the team knew that Nimba County community, business, and ministry leaders attended the school, they had no idea of the impact that the school was having after only two years of operation.

During their stay, the team heard the testimonies and visited the workplaces or ministries of five LICC students. The team saw firsthand how LICC students, through leadership roles in their professions and their ministries, are actively bringing hope and reconciliation to the Liberian people by sharing God's love as told through the Gospels, and by sacrificially serving the needs of the Liberian people. Their LICC education was equipping them with management and technical skills needed to do their jobs and minister to people more effectively. This has positively impacted hundreds, if not thousands of Liberians.

## Long-Term Needs of LICC

Please pray for these positions to be filled. If the job description fits you, ask God how He can use you.

**Business Professors:** These people would teach college-level business courses for a semester, a year, or multiple semesters. A Master's in business or experience teaching business courses at the college level is desired.

**Biblical Language Professors:** These people would teach Greek or Hebrew for one or more semesters.

**Various Other Professors:** We are open to varying lengths of time. We need instructors for courses in theology, Christian education, philosophy, sociology, and math.

## Short-Term Mission Trips

We have opportunities for short term mission trips to Liberia and LICC that range from 10 to 14 days. We provide accommodations, meals, and local transportation at reasonable costs. These trips are also designed to give you a *taste of the culture.*

Typical activities for short-term mission trips include teaching in the classroom, teaching Sunday School or Vacation Bible School to children, construction work, agricultural work like planting beans or fruit trees, and even evangelism outreach to local villages.

On a trip, we hope to create a safe and challenging place for you to grow in your love for Jesus. We also want you to become more aware of your own role in God's Kingdom as you build relationships with other team members. Most of our trips partner with people that are already launched into God's Kingdom revolution, so we hope that you add value to the amazing Kingdom work that is already taking place in Liberia. Lastly, we hope you experience more of God's Kingdom and that it changes you.

Delegation from Indiana on a Short-Term Trip

On a short term trip, you are potentially launching into a life-changing experience. Short-term trips are difficult, challenging, exhilarating, humbling, awe-inspiring, memorable, community-building, norm-defying, culture-shifting, and faith-building. Through a trip, you will become aware of some characteristics of God that up to now have been hidden from you. You will become more aware of who you are, and perhaps some of your own brokenness. You will become more aware of the amazing diversity that God has designed on His planet earth that reflects Him. You will become more aware of the desperate need for God's Kingdom.

## Our Needs in the United States

**Vision Partners:** These are friends who share in our vision, pursue our mission, and give regularly from the wealth God has given them to achieve the mission. *Everyone* can be a vision partner, as every gift is a sacrificial gift for God's Kingdom.

**Champions:** These people can be located anywhere in the United States, but work to connect us with North American supporters to meet our needs for expertise, financial resources, and prayer. Each gift to LICC is used for its intended purpose as designated by the originator. These people would need to be familiar with various types of funding, networking, or developing partnerships.

**Scholarships Coordinator**: This U.S.-based person would match students who need funding to an individual, several individuals, or an organization that desires to sponsor or help a student at the college.

**Faculty Development Coordinator**: This person would match a selected faculty member with funding from individuals or an organization that desire to sponsor a faculty member at the college to cover salary or for the faculty member to pursue advanced studies.

If you are interested in learning more about any of these opportunities with LICC, or have other ideas of ways you can contribute your gifts and talents, please contact me so we can discuss the possibilities:

Dr. Sei Buor
fsbuor1@gmail.com
ULICAF
P. O. Box 1158
Carmel IN 46082

# About the Authors

Dr. Sei and Yah Buor

Dr. Buor is a co-founder of the United Liberia Inland Church Associates & Friends located in Noblesville, Indiana. He is also the co-founder and President of the Liberia International Christian College in Ganta, Nimba County, Liberia. Dr. and Mrs. Buor have devoted their lives to furthering the cause of education within a Christian context in their Liberian homeland. The Buors live in Noblesville, Indiana, and Ganta, Liberia, and have five grown children who live in the United States.

Dr. Buor uses the story of LICC to encourage Christians everywhere in the value of steadfast faith and adherence to Christian principles as they pursue the visions that God has laid on their own hearts. If you would like to contact Dr. Buor for speaking engagements, please use the following:

Dr. Sei Buor
fsbuor1@gmail.com
ULICAF
P. O. Box 1158
Carmel IN 46082

Mark Oehler

Born and raised in the Seattle-area, Mark Oehler graduated with a degree in mechanical engineering from the University of Washington. While in college he became a Christian. Mark has spent most of his 30–plus year career writing manuals, procedures, and training. Mark resides in Central Indiana with his wife Nicole who shares his love for outdoor activities like hiking, backpacking, canoeing, and cross country skiing.

Mark met Sei Buor through a mutual friend. He helped edit Sei's first book, *NO MORE WAR*, so it was natural for Sei to enlist his help in researching and writing parts of this book.

Made in the USA
Middletown, DE
08 July 2015